Farewell Recital

Farewell Recital
Further Memoirs

Gerald Moore

HAMISH HAMILTON · London

First published in Great Britain 1978
by Hamish Hamilton Limited
90 Great Russell Street London WC1B 3PT

Second impression April 1978

Copyright © 1978 by Gerald Moore

British Library Cataloguing in Publication Data

Moore, Gerald, b. 1899
    Farewell recital.
    1. Moore, Gerald, b. 1899   2. Pianists—Biography
    I. Title
    786.1'092'4   ML417.M85
ISBN 0-241-89817-x

Printed and bound in Great Britain by
REDWOOD BURN LIMITED
Trowbridge & Esher

To Enid

Contents

List of Illustrations

Acknowledgments

I would like to thank the following friends: Martin Cooper for his generous contribution to my notes on *Music Magazine* and Philip Hope-Wallace on the same subject; Winifred Radford for allowing me to quote her translation from Pierre Bernac's *Interpretation of French Song* (Cassell & Co. Ltd.); Bernard Levin for sending me the cartoon from the *Sunday Express*; Edward Greenfield for the extensive quotation from his article on the sleeve of my Birthday Record; David Cairns' thoughts on *Rubato* from the *Sunday Times*; Geoffrey Parsons for the laughing picture at the playback of *Cats' Duet* and Madeleine Uggla of Stockholm.

Although I have not quoted the late Richard Capell, his book *Schubert's Songs* (Ernest Benn Ltd.) has for many years been an inspiration.

To my English publishers Hamish Hamilton Ltd. (Hamish Hamilton, Roger Machell, Julia MacRae) and my German publishers Rainer Wunderlich Verlag (the late Prof., Dr. Hermann Leins and Isabel Leins) I am deeply grateful for their constant interest and encouragement.

Farewell Recital

'HOW CAN we arrange things so that at Gerald's entry he can have special applause for himself?'

The question put by Walter Legge was addressed to his wife Elisabeth Schwarzkopf, to Victoria de los Angeles and to Dietrich Fischer-Dieskau. We had met for the last rehearsal before my Farewell Concert at the Royal Festival Hall. It would be an affectation if I glossed over this concert with reticence; it was one of the great days of my life.

For an accompanist to have a farewell appearance on such a scale was at least a rarity, perhaps even unprecedented, and for me to feel flattered was surely understandable. Flattered yes, but not out of proportion; others before me were more than worthy to have been similarly flattered—Hamilton Harty, Harold Craxton for instance—but there was no Walter Legge in the environs in their heyday. To state that I was made the central figure at this concert on February 20, 1967, hardly smacks of modesty and I am well aware that the presence of this illustrious trio of singers on the same stage was enough to fill the hall ten times over—so I have no illusions. I have only gratitude to my dear friends who came from Switzerland, Spain and Germany to do honour to me and to Walter Legge whose idea it was.

In the summer of 1965 I told a few friends in the artists' room at the Mozarteum after a Fischer-Dieskau recital that this was my last public appearance at the Salzburg Festival. I made this announcement—or rather I heard myself saying it—without premeditation. I kept my word. Fischer-Dieskau and Elisabeth Schwarzkopf, for whom I had played for so many recitals at the Mozarteum, were incredulous and, after realizing I meant it, not a little upset; it would have been more considerate of me to have taken them into my confidence, but my excuse, and a valid one, was that I made this decision on the spur of the moment. Enid, my wife, was as surprised as my friends.

It was in the months that followed that Walter Legge, founder of the

Philharmonia Orchestra, recording manager for E.M.I. for many years, was inspired to organize a Gerald Moore Farewell Concert in London. He took the entire operation into his own hands, booking the hall, arranging a date that would find these three artists in the same continent on the same night, deciding on ticket prices, making decisions as to recording and broadcasting the performance (the B.B.C. wanted to televise it, but Legge, after talking it over with me, rightly decided that it was unfair to a public buying expensive seats to be subjected for two hours to the discomfort of blazing lights.) Then there was the question of programme. The duets and trios were chosen with care and with imagination by Walter, only Rossini's *Cats' Duet* (*Duetto Buffo di due Gatti*) was, strangely, unknown to him. I must add that the effect of its performance at this concert with Elisabeth and Victoria was sensational.

No trouble was experienced in planning Elisabeth's solo group—it would of course consist of Hugo Wolf—where Schwarzkopf of all singers is supreme and whose songs, championed by her husband for more years than I can remember, are the love of his life. One wonders if Wolf with all his genius would have been recognized at his true worth today without the devoted energy of Legge, with his intimate knowledge of all Wolf's output. It was he who—inspired to inaugurate the Hugo Wolf Society through E.M.I's record volumes which he supervised and produced and for which he procured the world's best singers and accompanists—was largely responsible for spreading propaganda for Wolf throughout the world. So Schwarzkopf's solo group spoke for itself.

At my request, I believe, Dietrich Fischer-Dieskau's contribution was to be Franz Schubert. This was apt, for at that very period he and I were engaged on the vast undertaking of recording all the Schubert *Lieder* and Dieter was more than willing. For years we had been working at and performing Schubert together and hearing him sing these divine songs and partnering him in them was life-enhancing.

Now we were confronted with a problem, namely: how to get the particulars of Victoria de los Angeles' solo group. This deserves a paragraph on its own.

I have loved Victoria and played for her for many years, but the difficulty is this: her personal manager is her husband Enrique Magriña (whose vigilant watchword is *mañana*) and Enrique in his turn employed a secretary who was paid to destroy all correspondence unopened. I have yet to meet anyone who received a letter from Enrique and over all the period I played for Victoria I never succeeded in getting details of a programme, which I was longing to practise, until a few days before the recital. So what, in this particular exigency was Walter Legge to do? Of course in his innocence he wrote many times with the usual response—I should say result. He solved the problem in a way that is typical of his character, by a special expedition to Barcelona; it took a day or two, it took trouble, and he was put to some expense, but he got Victoria's programme—a group of Brahms songs. (I secretly wished they had been Spanish songs which I and her public adore and in which she feels so much at home, but I was too relieved and astonished that Victoria's group was decided upon to demur.) I had no idea that Walter had had to go to all this exertion, and assumed it was another of his miracles—but he always modestly admits that the miracles take a little longer!

Perhaps I should make it clear at this moment that this last appearance of mine was not a benefit concert in aid of the accompanist. It was advertised as 'Homage to Gerald Moore' and I have no doubt whatever that my three dear friends would have been happy to give their services and pour all the proceeds into my lap, but I would have none of it. True, we shared equally the royalties accruing from the recordings and the fees of the various radio transmissions, but I insisted that the friends with whom I had enjoyed so many thrilling hours and extensive tours should receive their full fees.

John Denison, then manager of the Royal Festival Hall, telephoned me one month before the concert to say, 'I thought you would be interested to know that the Box Office for your concert opened one hour ago and the hall is already sold out, and the queue goes all round the block.'

But to answer the question posed at the beginning of this modest essay about my entry. First it was suggested that the two ladies with me between them and Dieter following should process on to the platform, but Elisabeth said, 'Do you really want Gerald to have his own separate applause? Then this is the way to do it; we three singers walk out together and when the clapping which greets us has subsided Gerald walks out on his own.' It was a master stroke. I stood behind the curtain and waited like an old pro, like an old showman, for the applause which had greeted my friends to subside. I waited for complete silence and then I emerged.

Now this was a moment I had been preparing or arming myself for for some weeks. Suppose I was so moved that I could not control my emotion! I was reminded with a shudder how a friend celebrated his seventieth birthday by giving a dinner party for twenty guests. He had prepared a little speech, but when the moment came to make it he wept so unrestrainedly that his wife had to make it in his stead. We guests witnessed his heaving shoulders with averted eyes, embarrassed. What would this poor fellow have done before not a score but a multitude? I was determined that when the crucial moment came I would be in control of myself, but even so I was not prepared for what was in store. I walked out slowly with my eyes on the platform where I could see Elisabeth, Victoria and Dieter leading the applause. I turned to the public when I arrived centre stage and saw to my everlasting wonder that they were all on their feet. This sort of thing can be taken in its stride by Toscanini, Paderewski, Klemperer, Janet Baker (who experienced it in the very month when I am writing this) but a standing ovation for an artist is rare in England, and for an accompanist so unheard of that I was stirred to my soul, although remaining outwardly impassive. I turned quickly and embraced each of my three beloveds and then tottered to the piano stool.

In fact I was shaken and the recording shows in the first group of Mozart vocal trios that the pianoforte was far too faint, a reticence on my part not altogether due to my emotion. The imperfect balance was of course my fault, owing I think, to the fact that we had never rehearsed these trios except in a confined studio. The recording was under the direction of Suvi Raj Grubb, one of the chief recording managers of E.M.I. and the operator was Christopher Parker. Grubb told me that Daniel Barenboim was with him in the recording room attached to the hall and after the first trio he cried 'But Gerald is supposed to retire *after* the concert: he must have retired already because I can't hear him'.

The programme was beautifully planned. Two groups of vocal trios by Mozart and Haydn, two groups of duets in which Dieter sang Schumann with Elisabeth, Mendelssohn with Victoria and then each sang a solo group as I mentioned earlier.

By no means least was the group of three Rossini duets sung by the two ladies. The first of these—*La Regata Veneziana* tells of the nervous strain experienced by two girls as they watch their gondolier-lovers racing on the canal. 'Row, row, Tony' calls one. 'O dear Beppe is sweating and tiring' screams the other. I am afraid my sweeping arpeggios high in the treble and the swing of my right arm (a little higher swing than was strictly necessary) in an arc to land on a very very low note in the bass—caused some amusement, more especially as my mien was serious and concentrated for I was anxious about poor Beppe catching a crab and missing the right note.

But if this was amusing it was as nothing compared to Rossini's *Cats'*
Duet, where there are no words. The mewing and caterwauling, the
expressions on the faces of the singers—both consummate actresses—
as they 'mi-owed' in various degrees of intensity had the audience in an
uproar. What was to be said on the programme about this effusion?
Here is what is written:

> The text of this musical masterpiece is so subtle and allusive that
> no translation could do justice to the variety of the vocabulary.
> To-night's singers have promised that every syllable will be
> completely audible and intelligible.

This gem is unsigned but it is authentic Walter Legge.

From this programme, made up of such a rich mélange of superb
music, it is hard to say which groups gave me personally the most
pleasure. Perhaps I would pick the Schubert, Brahms and Wolf solo
songs, for I was intimate with them and had performed them countless
times with my partners. Victoria was under some disadvantage, for her
Brahms songs immediately followed the racket of the feline duet and
she had no time to rest or readjust the voice. But she took it as it came,
with professional equanimity or, as we English would say 'like a
sport'.

Elisabeth was in her most scintillating form but, aware that she was
being recorded, was always prepared to be dissatisfied with herself.
This is typical. At a recording session (not to be confused with a public
performance) she would disregard her first 'take' no matter how
beautifully she had sung it, on the principle that the more she sang the
lied the better it would be. So often the first effort would be the best
when the voice was fresh, but so self-critical is she that this possibility
was unacceptable to her in spite of Walter's and my efforts to convince
her. Listening to the Schwarzkopf group of Wolf played back to us
after the concert she was unhappy, but Fischer-Dieskau said he could
not conceive a more glorious performance of these songs. Great
artists are rarely pleased with themselves, Fischer-Dieskau, master that
he is, takes things philosophically and has often said of his work, 'It is
not good but it is the best I can do.'

John Denison was concerned lest the Artists' Room would be
swamped with people when the concert was over and at his suggestion
when I addressed the public (prefacing my remarks with the words
'Pray be seated' for again they had stood) to thank them for nearly half
a century of kindness to me, I added 'It is possible that a goodly number

of you will want to come back stage and greet Elisabeth Schwarzkopf, Victoria de los Angeles and Dietrich Fischer-Dieskau. Some of you may even want to see the back of me but the management say that if you obey this impulse the hall will not be able to shut its doors till the early hours of the morning and these wonderful singers will lose their last buses home. Let me say my good-bye and express my gratitude with the help of Franz Schubert'.

I played the first verse of *An die Musik*.

The concert was over and I walked off the stage forever and without a pang.

Miau or Miaow

THE RECORD issued separately on a 45 r.p.m. that Elisabeth Schwarzkopf and Victoria de los Angeles made of the *Cats' Duet* together with *La Regata Veneziana* swept the world. Since the performance I have had so many letters asking me for information respecting it that I gladly supply it: the full and majestic title is *Duetto Buffo di due Gatti* (Comic Duet for Two Cats), its composer is G. Rossini and the publishers are Peters.

Quite a lot of music has been inspired by cats: there is the *Cat's Fugue* by Scarlatti inspired by his pet walking on the keyboard; Stravinsky wrote *Three Cats' Lullabies* and in *L'enfant et les Sortilèges* Ravel has a duet for cats; Tchaikovsky's *Sleeping Beauty* has a *pas de deux* for them.

As for the duet under discussion—(surely written *by* cats and *for* cats though ascribed to Rossini) it only seemed to impinge on the public ear comparatively recently. Elisabeth Söderstrom and Kirsten Mayer introduced it to me at Aldeburgh where it almost caused a riot. A recording of it was made by Christa Ludwig and Walter Berry.

Elisabeth's and Victoria's characterization, the occasional sly expression on their faces, their sulky menacing *miau* (English cats would say 'miaow' but these were Italian) rising to a caterwauling screech, took me by surprise, as there had been no evidence of histrionics at rehearsal, and my equilibrium at the keyboard was considerably and pleasantly disturbed.

In a footnote in the score Robin de Smet tells us that Rossini had to imitate the sound of a cat every morning at three outside the house of his mistress so that she could recognize him and let him in.

Thus was the masterpiece inspired. De Smet concludes with the exhortation 'May the best performer win!'

The Order of Your Going

ALTHOUGH I had said goodbye in London, I had a further commitment ahead of me, for twelve months previously I had promised Fischer-Dieskau to go in this same season to America for two recitals in New York and one in Washington. It was particularly pleasing to me to pay my last respects to the Carnegie Hall; I have always found it warm and friendly. The many artists who love it are grateful to Isaac Stern who was largely responsible for preserving it from demolition.

Dieter (I am tempted to say, as usual) had a triumph but with the unselfishness of the great, made me precede him on to the platform and presented me with a bouquet.

But *he* preceded *me* out of Washington after the Sunday afternoon concert there. To my amusement he disappeared like lightning as soon as he could escape because he said 'I must catch the next flight to New York to hear Ella Fitzgerald and Duke Ellington this evening as I may never get another chance to hear them together'. I mention this as an instance of Fischer-Dieskau's insatiable hunger and all-embracing taste for music no matter what the style.

And now I may be asked 'How many farewells are you going to make?' This was the question thrown at John McCormack at a press reception to publicize his last recital at the Royal Albert Hall in 1938.

I attended that affair though my presence was quite unnecessary, but I had the furtive hope—never to be disclosed—that I might be mentioned as 'among those present was the well-known etc. etc.' In fact I was unnoticed. The reporters made themselves free at the cocktail bar—here I was fairly prominent—until the entry of the hero of the occasion who sat himself at a long table covered with green baize like a billiard table and was at once surrounded by his guests with their notebooks who shouldered me aside without compunction. Yes, pushed out of the way or, to carry the billiard-room simile a step further I found myself pocketed or at best in baulk. Questions were showered on McCormack which he brushed aside without trouble. The thought of slinking away crossed my mind when, the catechism having made a decided *diminuendo e rallentando*, a voice was heard clearly asking, 'Count McCormack, which is your favourite of all the songs you are going to sing next Sunday afternoon?' 'Without a doubt it is Hugo Wolf's *Herr was trägt der Boden hier?* (Lord, What will Grow in this Ground?)' was the unhesitating reply. 'And what does that mean?' There was an unaccustomed and painful silence which lasted too long when I suddenly heard the anguished cry of 'Jurrl, Jurrl' (to rhyme with 'churl'—John's way of pronouncing my Christian name.) For a fleeting moment the spotlight was on me as I provided the translation (in retrospect, it was just as well after all that I was there as a stop-gap. This embarrassing lapse of John's was never mentioned by either of us afterwards!) What might seem to have been a humiliating contretemps was quickly forgotten when John was asked, 'How many times are you going to give farewell concerts?'

How many farewells?

I was reminded of this after my farewell evening described in the opening chapter, for within a short time we had offers to repeat the concert with the same programme and artists in Paris, Berlin, Munich, New York and Los Angeles. But I was in no doubt whatever that my *congé* was final. A reappearance would make me feel like an old circus horse hungering for the feel of the sawdust under him and for the applause that greeted his old well-worn tricks. It is incredible, now my retirement is well known, that I have since had innumerable offers to re-emerge and it convinces me that the farewell idea is now regarded as a gimmick, one's departure from the scene to be made by degrees. After the official farewell (for which all your friends have bought tickets in good faith) there comes a prudent interval to be followed by a 'final appearance' and then a 'positively last', by which time your fans begin to realize they are being taken for a ride.

Now no more concert tours—no more insomnia worrying about my fourth finger.

Eugene Goossens said, 'There are only two difficult things in conducting, one is to start the orchestra and the other is to stop it.' It is not easy for the individual artist to know exactly when to stop. My dear Elena Gerhardt knew how to do it: true she went on singing in public a little longer than she should, though there was always something to be learned from her. We had an engagement in Liverpool and a few days before, she telephoned, 'I particularly want you to bring Enid with you.' At Euston we saw with pleasure that Dr. Fritz Kohl, her husband, was in our party and I asked Elena 'Why Enid and Fritz?' 'Because my

dear Jerry, this is going to be my last recital.' There were no preliminary announcements or tearful embraces in the artists' room after
the concert, we all returned to the Adelphi and had an hilarious
champagne supper.

That king of pianists Artur Rubinstein, venerated by all musicians—
with a panache I have never heard equalled by contemporary pianists
—went on a fraction too long. It was wonderful to witness the vitality
of an octogenarian dashing off Chopin's A flat Polonaise (the unbelievable miracle of those thundering octaves in the bass) as an encore
after performing two pianoforte concertos. But I found myself hoping
that he would not—yet again—respond to our applause with the same
Polonaise when I next heard him. He did. It was a little too much, not
for him but for me. One gets tired of being confounded.

But, like Gerhardt, when Rubinstein was no longer at his zenith
there was so much to take to heart, his Chopin C sharp minor study
(Op. 10 no. 4) where the crystal clear speed of the semi-quavers in the
treble was to be expected, but not the marvellously casual left hand
accompaniment—almost insolent in its relaxation. Fascinating! Again
in C sharp minor—the Valse (Op. 64 no. 2): the questioning hesitation
of the first two bar phrase to be put at rest by the delicate *rubato* answer
in the next two bars. *Auch kleine Dinge können uns entzücken*: it is the
little things recalled with so much pleasure that make me grateful to
Rubinstein rather than the derring-do.

I first heard Maria Callas at the Edinburgh Festival in Bellini's *La
Sonnambula* and within two minutes of her entry was deeply moved by
her singing. More than the quality of her tone, the nuance of her
phrases so felicitously shaped brought tears to my eyes—this was in her
recitative long before she had reached her aria, moments never to be
forgotten—and I still relate her infinitely sensitive phrasing to that of
Fritz Kreisler. The thrills of her matchless *coloratura*—*Norma*, *Lucia di
Lammermoor* and the rest followed season after season. I heard her in
opera for the last time at Covent Garden in *Tosca*. She was the greatest
singing actress of her time and although her voice was past its best, all
who heard her second act still talk about it. We watched spell-bound
when the gradual and fearful comprehension of possible deliverance
slowly dawned on her as her eyes fell on the carving knife on the supper
table—its stealthy grasp—the approach of Scarpia—the sudden turn
and fatal stabbing (done with such violence that Tito Gobbi, the
Scarpia, told me that at the stage business of placing the candles at the
head and feet of the corpse Callas whispered to him 'I hope I did not
hurt you'.)

Why after a career of historical triumph in opera and having lain fallow for some years did Mme Callas conceive the idea of a come-back, of a world tour of concerts with pianoforte accompaniment? It was not her *métier*. She emerged on to the platform of the Royal Festival Hall looking regal in a gown fit for a queen. With Giuseppe Di Stefano as escort she processed round and round acknowledging the rapturous acclamation of her adorers, and it must be confessed there was an aura about the Callas presence that seemed to put her audience in a frenzy. It was reminiscent, I thought, of the reappearance of Ignaz Jan Paderewski following the 1914–18 war after he had been Poland's President, or the return of the legendary violoncellist Pablo Casals in 1945. No doubt these recollections would not have entered my head had I been in the Hall; the excitement might have been contagious, but as it happened I was viewing proceedings on the tele-vision—and at this moment I was called to the telephone. When I returned to give the music my full attention I found, to my astonish-ment, that the artists were still turning and bowing to all points of the compass; on and on they went in a sort of pavan, majestic, unendingly repetitive. Not a note had yet been heard. Would the applause never cease? Paderewski or Casals would have terminated it with a gesture—and in any case the twisting and turning would have made them dizzy. It dawned on me that these gyrations were part of the show. I wondered what was passing through Ivor Newton's mind as he sat at his keyboard waiting for the clamour to subside: to him fell the un-rewarding task of accompanying operatic arias and duets with their oom-pah-pahs on the pianoforte, when, if ever, the diva decided to sing. Sing at long last she did and was but a shadow of her former self. One felt sorry she had been persuaded to expose herself in this way. The most reliable performer of the evening was Ivor who accompanied inscrutably.

One must be content to cry 'Enough' and leave it at that.

Elisabeth Schwarzkopf, still more beautiful than any singer has a right to be, gave in an interview an answer which every artist should take to heart. 'How can I announce a Farewell Recital when my very next concert may be my last?'

Whither?

MY RETIREMENT prompted indignant response from many musicians, the great Pablo Casals asked with some heat what was I thinking about? His twin, the equally youthful nonagenarian Lionel Tertis, also a dear friend, shook his head sadly for what he called my foolishness. Strangely enough artists with whom I had never been associated asked me to appear with them—Gregor Piatigorsky, to play the Beethoven Violoncello Sonatas in London and Paris, Grace Bumbry to tour in recitals, Peter Schreier the German tenor and others.

Perhaps it seems unreasonable that at the comparatively early age of sixty-seven I should forsake the concert platform, but I had been a professional accompanist for over fifty years and I felt a change would be good for me, moreover I had other ideas at the back of my mind. Was my wish for a change provoked by nervous strain? It was not. Of course I suffered from nervousness before and during a performance, no less and no more acutely than most artists I know, but I never felt the strain was unendurable, or the responsibility too much to bear.

Responsibility! What strain there was is summed up in that single word. Here the soloist and the accompanist are in different categories for the former is only responsible to himself. Paderewski was once asked after a recital if he had played any wrong notes. 'Any?' was the reply, 'I played enough wrong notes to make a new composition.' Laugh as he may have done, the great Polish pianist was so nervous before a recital that he had to be coaxed on to the platform. He was obsessed with the fear of wrong notes. Every pianist carries this obsession to extremes; our instrument may not be so formidable to master as the string players' but we have a multitude of notes to cover.

Emanuel Feuermann, that most immaculate of 'cellists, laughed when we were returning to our hotel after a concert, 'I was not very good this evening,' and he seemingly dismissed it from his mind.

Nobody else recognized that he was not in his best form but *he* knew it and philosophically laughed it off. (All the same I heard him sweating away on his 'cello like the devil incarnate the following morning in his bedroom.)

Responsibility! I joined Elisabeth Schwarzkopf and Dietrich Fischer-Dieskau at the Carnegie Hall for a performance of Hugo Wolf's *Italienisches Liederbuch* (Italian Song Book), a work which I have loved and lived with for many years and had played often with these and other artists. It was my first appearance in New York for several seasons and I was given a warm welcome. The first song *Auch kleine Dinge können uns entzücken* (Even Little Things Can Delight Us) is a tranquil and charming song, much more of a test for a singer at the beginning of a recital than for the accompanist. What happened? In my simple introduction consisting of four bars, I marred the lovely tune in my left hand with an inexcusable smudged note. 'Forget about it—put it behind you for God's sake' is the thought, but it is a shattering moment and you try to recover from it as soon as can be. You are like the ice-skater in a dance pairs competition with a four-minute programme who in the first half minute has a fall. At once he knows he has let his partner down; at once he knows he cannot get high marks; at once he knows that his bloomer is apparent to the veriest ignoramus in the audience: he fights with himself to regain his concentration, his poise, to win back some semblance of confidence.

If you suggested to the judges who are to award marks that they should take the unfortunate ice-skater's nervousness into consideration they would look very coldly at you.

Should the music critic, a human being with imagination, likewise be expected to observe the same saving clause? No, he naturally reviews what he hears on the evidence of his ears and mind.

Every time he steps on to the stage the musician is giving a first performance. He may have played Wolf's *Italian Song Book* or Mozart and Beethoven sonatas almost to his own satisfaction two days previously but that is over, past recall: can he maintain the same standard this evening? He practises most of the day with diligence, forces himself to take a short siesta, arrives at the hall rested and full of hope, perhaps a little strung up but not so much as he was the day before yesterday. And then? He plays like a pig. (Of course I am referring to myself).

I know I have acquired a reputation as a good accompanist but I must admit that I am well aware of occasions when I have let my partner down. Possibly my colleague did not realize I was off colour, that I could have been more of an inspiration; but *I* knew. Being a professional I would not rush up to him wringing my hands in self-condemnation.

'You accompanists are never nervous' is a hackneyed phrase with which I have been regaled fairly frequently; it was an assertion, not a question and may have been intended as a compliment. I did not like it and was annoyed because my appearance is not suggestive of the sensitive poetic artist; I felt it could have been expressed quite accurately by the words 'You accompanists are automatons' or 'You fellows are bovine'. Naturally we endeavour to look self-possessed (it is for the prima-donna or her husband to have tantrums) and conduct ourselves with due consideration for our partner, who would hardly feel secure if she saw us looking thoroughly frightened. We walk on to the platform pretending we are absolutely sure of ourselves—how else should we look?

Your true musician, for all the assurance he exudes in public, is generally a modest man; the more serious and reverential his approach to his art the more aware is he that he is walking on a tightrope. Even Jascha Heifetz, of all musicians of my time the most flawless executant, accepted that some measure of insecurity existed. Nobody on this earth has perfect control.

Heifetz, nearly two years my junior, retired from concert playing not so long after I did. But his life's passion could not be abandoned: violinists flock to him from the end of the world to his workshop. When they emerge they bear the Heifetz stamp: I know because I have played for some of them.

But the question now arises—whither? I said earlier that I had other ideas at the back of my mind. For some years I had been active (apart from writing one or two books in my spare time) in three different spheres of music: Recording, to which I was initiated in 1922 and which was to become the vertebral column of my professional life; Lecture Recitals beginning at the National Gallery, Trafalgar Square in 1940; and lastly, giving me almost my greatest pleasure, my Master Classes for singers and accompanists which first saw the light of day in Sweden in 1962.

To these three interests then, I would now be able to devote all my time.

Since the reader also has a right to know whither he is being led, I assure him that my heart-felt wish is to treat him with every consideration, to cosset him to the utmost so that my leaps from one century to another (for it is as well to remind him that the writer has the honour of being a Victorian) and back again as if he were a yo-yo, do not make him dizzy.

The different streams of my activity naturally overlap one another but my aim is to treat each of them separately and as chronologically as possible. Inevitably there are various back-waters off the main stream at which I want to peep. I only hope they will not be regarded as dead-ends. For instance in my next chapter I would like to describe in general terms the experience and growth of a youth anxious to make a career as an accompanist, groping his way forward and occasionally losing balance.

Weighed in the Balance

AM I TOO loud? is a question that is or ought to be in the mind of an ensemble pianist at all times. Even the solo pianist has to consider the balance of tone between the hands, but he has the advantage that his right hand knows what his left hand is doing, though this is not to be taken for granted as is evidenced when he is incapable of synchronizing them in a simple chord. Naturally the problem comes more urgently to the attention when the composition involves two performers.

My earliest days, after I had emerged from the dismal embraces of Gurlitt and Loeschhorn, were spent with Czerny exercises and Bach Preludes and Fugues, and the routine was varied when I played violin sonatas with a fellow student.

I apologize for taking the reader back nearly seventy years—1 know 'the world is waiting for the sunrise' but it is a gradual process.

As a youngster of fifteen years of age I found myself in a trio with violin and 'cello in a small down-town picture theatre in Toronto. This was in the silent screen days, prior to my graduation to the bleating *vox humana* and giant palpitations of an organ in a larger cinema. My colleagues, very much my senior, were serious musicians, *manqués*, and we enjoyed ourselves hugely by playing—or rather playing at— Beethoven, Brahms trios and the like, scrambling through an entire work regardless of what was happening on the silver screen, ploughing on despite wrong notes or false entries. We were well aware we were not quite in the Cortot-Thibaud-Casals class; in fact we agreed that 'our playing yesterday of the Beethoven Archduke Trio was so bad we must leave it alone to ripen'. It was in the course of another superb work that the manager sped down the centre gangway and leaning over the brass rail separating us from the audience, hissed, 'What the flaming hell is that lousy tune you're playing?' 'It is by Beethoven,' our violinist answered, not without dignity. 'Look at the screen, look at the screen' and we obeyed and beheld Red Indians on the warpath encircling pale faces in their covered wagons. As accompaniment to this scene of frightful carnage we had been playing with intense concentration and oblivious of mundane considerations, the slow movement of the Ghost Trio. I was going to say that it was all done to earn an honest penny—but it was not so honest because we cheated the man who insulted Beethoven. Our leader would look up on occasion at the screen and quietly call 'Moonlight'—this meant the first movement of the Beethoven Sonata Op. 27 no. 2 (arranged as a trio!) whose strains went to a 'death-bed' sequence or a heart-rending farewell. Another favourite adaptation would be the *Allegretto* from the seventh Symphony, accessory to a nocturnal house-breaking, so mysterious, so stealthy. Beethoven would not have been pleased, but he helped us through the dark hours.

From these innocent diversions I was promoted to a partnership with Jan and Boris Hambourg, violinist and 'cellist. The latter eventually took me on a Canadian tour with a tenor as assisting artist.

This was my first experience of playing for a singer apart from accompanying friends at home; the idea of drowning them with our modest upright piano never entered my mind, especially as they stood looking over my shoulder at the music and nearly bellowed my head off. But accompanying a singer on a concert grand pianoforte with my partner some feet away was a different proposition and on this tour I began to realize that I had to adjust myself to a different balance.

At a public performance or rehearsal violinists and 'cellists place themselves very close to their partner on the keyboard side and the pianist hears their tone directly, whereas the singer standing in the bend of the piano directs her voice into the auditorium and he will not hear her with the immediacy and certainty that he heard the strings. This is not the end of the matter. While responsibility for obtaining a just balance is shared in a violin or 'cello sonata, in a song recital the onus rests on the accompanist who, until he gains experience, will reduce his tone in order to hear the voice clearly above the sound he himself is making: should he do this the tonal balance will be satisfactory to him but not so pleasing to the discriminating listener or to the singer, who will miss the support she needs.

I suggest that virtuoso artists of the greatest sensibility make this error of judgement in their early days of partnership with the voice. If justice is to be done to the grandeur of *Die Allmacht*, *Der Atlas*, *An schwager Kronos*, *Gruppe aus dem Tartarus*, Schubert's markings must be obeyed and if a *fortissimo* is demanded it must be given. True, only a whisper of the singer's voice will reach his ears (enough for him to know the two of them are attacking the same note at the same time) but an obvious reduction of tone is craven and only emasculates the thunderous songs I have quoted. To reconcile oneself to this false balance (it is no less) takes courage and experience and the player will be subjected to some criticism when things go wrong. But, speaking for myself, I would say however strongly I play I always hear the singer's voice *through* my tone, no matter how faint his sound may seem. No contradiction here.

'The *fortissimo* markings must be obeyed' I wrote in the last paragraph. One can see that my generalization is far too sweeping by glancing at the score of *Gruppe aus dem Tartarus*. (A Group in Tartarus).

Fischer-Dieskau in his *Biographical Study of Schubert Songs** writes of it 'The voice no longer has a "song melody", the action is depicted more by the harmonic and rhythmical audacities of the piano than by the song.' The scene is the bottomless pit of Tartarus: the moaning of the damned is heard: 'Over their heads eternity circles and shatters Saturn's sickle in twain'. After the subterranean rumbling of the pianoforte the volcano erupts with an explosion on the word *Ewigkeit* (Eternity) and five times the voice leaps down an octave. It is a mighty climax and the composer marks it *Fortissimo*. Each precise moment the vocal line drops like a stone down a well, the accompaniment leaps up in pitiless triumph and Schubert writes in the piano part *sforzando* reinforcing the *ff*. Is the pianist to obey? It cannot be done; he mercifully tempers his tone when the singer sinks below the stave but attempts to do so as subtly as possible: this can be achieved by a change of the sustaining pedal, so that the overtones on the resounding first syllable of *Ewigkeit* are released and he gives more emphasis to the *sforzando* in the bass octave in the left hand at the expense of his treble.

The ghastly picture of these damned souls in torment does not inspire lovely sounds; the pianist as much as the singer seeks to describe the horror of it. Chromatic heavings and sinkings at that ominous start of the song portend damnation; the darkness of the pit can be sensed by the turbid writing, it is to be over-pedalled and muddy, surging as an evil and opaque bubble for a moment and then bursting impotently and suddenly. To the dreadful answer 'Eternity' a beautiful tone from the pianoforte is unthinkable, it demands a harsh unyielding quality. Through all this hubbub from the pianoforte, the voice must be heard.

From this clamour out of ⌐he inferno let us contemplate a song of heavenly beatitude, Schubert with a full heart pouring forth his praise

* Cassell and Co., 1976.

to the Creator of life in *Die Allmacht*. Both songs by coincidence are in C major.

It was easy in *Gruppe aus dem Tartarus* for the pianist to get a steely sound in his climaxes, but now he wants weight and power without percussiveness: his tone must befit the occasion. He bears in mind the quality of the great organ. At the singer's words *Gross ist Jehovah, der Herr* the accompaniment is marked *piano* with a *crescendo*, and these instructions are duly observed: but the secret is in the use of the sustaining pedal. With this pedal firmly held down his tone can be increased enormously with little effort and with no crashing of hands on to the keys. The pedalling should not be clinically clean, for in a cathedral there is an inevitable acoustical overtone or echo. A voice of majestic power is needed to cope with this song.

Only on the rarest occasions does the composer deliberately ask for the voice to be smothered. I think immediately of Schubert's *Am Feierabend*, the fifth song in *Die Schöne Müllerin*. The miller lad sees the girl saying *Gute Nacht* to the assembled mill hands without even glancing in his direction, and his inner frustration is shown by the anger in the piano part. We hear 'Gute' but the '*Nacht*' is covered by the accompaniment's *subito forte*. (In truth there are many cases in Schubert's songs where the vocal line has a *pp* against the pianoforte's *piano*, or a *mezzo-forte* against the piano's *forte* but I think these are accidents attributable to Schubert's haste.)

At the close of Henri Duparc's *Phidylé*

> Que ton plus beau sourire et ton meilleur baiser
> Me récompensent de l'attente

the voice sinks down, passion spent: the pianoforte conversely soars to its biggest climax and 'de l'attente' is, unavoidably and rightly, eclipsed.

These are exceptional cases and not the order of the day. My recommendation that the voice must be heard by the player *through* the pianoforte's tone should be constantly borne in mind otherwise the accompanist will be unpopular.

'Normally the most considerate of accompanists, on this occasion Gerald Moore too often overwhelmed the singer' Martin Cooper wrote in the *Daily Telegraph*, and it was this criticism that suggested to me the title of my book *Am I too Loud?** But (and this is a confession I would never make had I not retired from the concert platform) I

* Hamish Hamilton, 1962.

would rather be guilty of being too loud than the reverse side of the coin. I well remember my first meeting and rehearsal with Emanuel Feuermann, that marvellous 'cellist; before we started to play he said, 'I have been told you are not too reticent in your playing.' Be that as it may we had a happy association for many years.

The violoncello has to be treated with discretion by the pianist for its lowest tones can easily be swamped by the pianoforte. After an Amaryllis Fleming recital, my friend Hamish Hamilton told me I was sometimes too loud for the 'cello, 'Or perhaps,' he added, 'Amaryllis was too soft for the pianoforte.'

Dame Myra Hess played often with the Griller Quartet and at one of their concerts at the Wigmore Hall she turned to the audience during the pause between movements and asked, 'Am I too heavy for the strings?' The audience was too surprised to want to start a discussion in the middle of a piece of music and in any case their judgement would have been unreliable.

Much depends, where balance is concerned, on the size of the voice or instrument for which you are playing. Elena Gerhardt at the beginning of our partnership begged me 'not to be too discreet'; Victoria de los Angeles also liked lots of support. The deeper voice— baritone or bass—like the 'cello has to be treated with consideration, but Fischer-Dieskau paid me the compliment, even in the most thunderous of songs, of trusting to my judgement.

1   Farewell Recital, 20 February 1967:
above: L. to r.: the author, Victoria de los Angeles, Elisabeth
Schwarzkopf, Dietrich Fischer-Dieskau.   *below:* The author

2 Dame Janet Baker

3   Master Classes:
above: Stockholm 1963
below: Tokyo, October 1965

4   *above :* Playback of the *Cats' Duet :* Dietrich Fischer-Dieskau, Enrique Magrina, Elisabeth Schwarzkopf, author, Victoria de los Angeles. *below :* Seventieth Birthday Record : Suvi Raj Grubb, Dame Janet Baker and author

Poem and Pianoforte

THE SINGER with the patience to read these lines will forgive me I hope, if following my observations on balance, I continue to pay more attention to the accompanist. It is not with the intention of giving the latter more importance at the expense of the singer, but because only a few master accompanists give their heart and their all in the composer's service. The singer is grateful to a partner who shares with him the burden of the song but it is he, I repeat, whose predominance is unquestioned; our eyes are on him for it is his physiognomy which reflects the mood or changing moods of what he is singing. We do not need to look at the accompanist at all, unless perhaps our eyes stray in his direction in an introduction, interlude, or postlude, but he is coming between the singer and the song if he draws attention to himself while his partner is giving voice. So far as the singer is concerned it must be agreed the eyes have it. The ears?

I attempt to show in one or two 'simple' songs altogether at variance with the massive songs in the foregoing chapter, how important it is that ears and mind should be opened equally to voice and piano, and I am taking three songs which illustrate this coalescence.

Discussing Hugo Wolf's *Anakreons Grab*, in *Singer and Accompanist* (*The Performance of Fifty Songs*)★ I wrote, 'Surely when Goethe recited these simple and tender lines it was in the same gentle rhythm, with the same stresses, inflexions, pauses, that Wolf has given us. I like to indulge in the notion that Goethe had this very music in mind when he wrote the little poem. If singer and accompanist will share my credulity it will not be unhelpful to their performance and it gives some indication of the almost miraculous fusion of words and music.'

The proposition that the rose-scented fragrance of a summer breeze can be suggested by the contact of fingers on the piano may seem fanciful but the accompanist has got to believe he can do it: after his introduction we should not be surprised that the singer's theme is

★ Methuen & Co., 1953.

2

nature's loveliness. 'Where the rose blooms, where vine and laurel are entwined' he sings, while the piano pictures the blooms and greenery with a falling cluster of notes in the treble played with refined freedom and delicately touched as if the flowers themselves were being caressed. Singer and pianist *see* the scene—they are part of it. 'What grave is here?' and 'It is Anakreon's' are moments of awe, subdued in tone, soon to be succeeded by rapture for the sanctuary adorned so bountifully by the gods for Anakreon's resting place. And finally as the voice is hushed the pianoforte postlude takes us gently by the hand to draw us away: we go with unwilling steps, and ever and anon turn our heads (the tied notes in the receding treble) to look again at the green mound where the poet lies.

Am I fooling myself? Am I living in cloud-cuckoo land? Let him who believes so give up all hope of being a worthy partner for the singer. His feeling for the word must be as deep and responsive as his partner's, acutely—not subconsciously—aware of it so that when he hears in Beethoven's *Adelaide* the singer devotedly breathe 'A-de-la-i-de' he himself *pronounces* the blessed name on the pianoforte keys. His mind and body are sharpened to the finest point of concentrated faith in and love of what he is doing and this consummation is transmitted through his fingers.

The solo pianist partnering the voice sometimes exercises authority that the too modest accompanist lacks. Let us take *Morgen* (Tomorrow) by Richard Strauss as an example. The introduction—half the length of the song—is the quintessence of tranquil serenity, it flows or rather floats seemingly without volition, so prolonged are the pauses and silences. This is the core of the song, the pivot round which the singer will later weave his mesmeric *obligato*. The mental poise to make these precious moments of immobility impressive finds the too timorous accompanist at a loss, he therefore curtails these pregnant resting points simply because his congenital modesty cannot support the burden of attention that is being focused on him. (*Le silence éternel de ses espaces infinis m'effraie* he will mutter to himself with that facility for *le mot juste* which comes so easily to accompanists even in an emergency). And this is where the authority of the virtuoso pianist is advantageous. The man who has communed with Beethoven in his slow movements —the Funeral March in the A flat major sonata (Op. 26) or the *Adagio sostenuto* of the Moonlight Sonata—is not going to be ill at ease with Richard Strauss. Undoubtedly in this song, serene and tender though it be, singer and pianist must exercise masterly restraint to give the long silences their full value. I grudgingly concede that on a record or broadcast the silences, if relentlessly held to their ordered length, create a vacuum; they need the living presence of the singer to hold the listener.

When playing this song I have relished the silences to which I refer above, but a study of the score reveals that there is hardly an instance where no tone is being sung or played. So often, however, at the fading tail-end of a phrase one small note in the soprano voice of the accompaniment is being held and is so attenuated that its tone will not survive until the end of the bar. If this is not tantamount to a silence, let me say that inevitably it causes moments of no sound—moments to be enjoyed without fear.

Morgen gives much pleasure to the listener because of its tenderness and by the sense of relaxation it exudes: paradoxically it calls for strength from the performers—the more so because it never rises above a *mezza voce*. The pianist evokes the mood, sets the pattern and shape by his playing of the introduction. He directs the course of the song.

There are occasions far more frequent than the average player is aware when the accompanist is in control. He will play the introduction of Schubert's *Ave Maria* with musical feeling perhaps, without realizing that the singer is fettered by the tempo he is establishing. And the singer is helpless since she can do nothing to alter the pace, for the simple reason that she holds long sustained notes and it is impossible for her to indicate that she wants the accompanist to get a move on. She listens with apprehension knowing that she cannot contain the two words of that long phrase in the essential single breath; the audience will hear 'A——ve'—then a quick heaving breath noticed by everybody—'Maria'. At a Promenade Concert at the Royal Albert Hall I stood very close to Elisabeth Schumann when she sang this song. She was a dear friend and we had worked so much together that I heard with dismay the accompanist setting far too slow a tempo. Her concern was unnoticed by the general public for she was too experienced a professional to betray herself, but I sensed her growing anxiety as she listened to the long introduction. She actually managed the huge phrase in one breath but it was a near thing and I know she suffered discomfort where a lesser singer would have been thrown. 'But, mein Schatz, did you hear *Ave Maria?*' she asked when I saw her some days later. I told her, 'I certainly did but nobody else had any suspicion of your suffering, least of all the accompanist who went home perfectly happy, in blissful ignorance that he had nearly asphyxiated you'—and as usual Elisabeth dismissed the event with laughter, having by this time recovered her breath.

Nacht und Träume (Night and Dreams) is another instance where the singer must rely on the pianist setting the rehearsed tempo. In *Gretchen am Spinnrade* (Gretchen at the Spinning Wheel) the tempo can be quickened or retarded at the voice's entry, for the vocal line has movement; the three notes on *Meine Ruh* are enough for a readjustment to be made: in *Doppelgänger* (The Shadow Double) again the first vocal phrase *Still ist die Nacht* will correct an erring accompanist. But these are emergency operations and the listener should be unaware of them. The player should feel some shame that he did not bear in mind the agreed tempo of each song at rehearsals.

Let us consider Claude Debussy's *La Chevelure* (The Tresses of Hair) the second song in the set of *Chansons de Bilitis*. In this, the pianist without empathy can abort the artistry of the most perceptive of singers; he must feel personally involved.

The pianoforte, with its soft sighing discords (not too strictly in tempo) speaks at once of femininity and introduces the girl who recalls with restrained but sensuous pleasure how her lover told her of his dreams. 'He said to me, "I dreamed the black tresses of your hair were circled about my neck and on my breast and I caressed them as if they were part of me, as if we were united ever thus, mouth upon mouth, like two laurels that have but one root".'

Voice and pianoforte at first are locked together in gentle languorous embrace; gradually the music increases in passion and quickens in pulse. At *Je les caressais* the accompaniment begins to have a life of its own as exemplified by the triplet figure in the treble, it seems to caress the vocal line. This freedom is even more in evidence at the two dynamic climaxes: the first *Par la même chevelure la bouche sur la bouche* sees the singer's soaring phrase complemented by the pianist's downsweep; it is marked *en pressant*, *sur la bouche* being the apex. Time must be allowed before the *piano subito* so that we can hear clearly what the singer says in this sudden drop of tone. A similar time allowance is necessary after the song's only *fortissimo*, *ou que tu entrais en moi comme mon songe*. Here the pianoforte's *fermata* is essential because now we hear—ever so softly—the sensuous, languid chords of the introduction presaging the most affecting moments of the song. To the same notes that the girl began *Il m'a dit* she now sings *Quand il eut achevé* (After this, he put his hands gently on my shoulders and looked at me so tenderly that I lowered my eyes with a shiver.) (*frisson*)

In *La Chevelure* Debussy gives us a key signature of six flats permitting us to know that the tonic key is G flat major or its relative E flat minor; uncertainty is prolonged before the music resolves or settles in the home key. Not until the twenty-fourth bar out of a total of twenty-seven, do we realize that the song is in G flat major though even here it carries an intrusive A flat in an inner voice. This beautiful and unruffled discord comes on the significant words '—*et il me regarda d'un regard si tendre*'. It is the emotional high-point of the song, the composer marks it *très pianissimo* and its soothing sound is dwelt on that we may appreciate it the more. (The fact that the tonic chord makes such a late appearance is not merely of academic interest, the artists must be acutely aware of it for they see the map of every song they perform in their minds' eye before they begin so that their course can be plotted, the high point—in the distance—anticipated.) Only once throughout the whole composition is the pure and simple common chord heard, this is when it arrives peacefully in G flat major on the very last chord.

Winifred Radford (whose brilliant translations are a feature of Pierre Bernac's *Interpretation of French Song**) says that Bilitis—a girl of fifteen or sixteen—is an imaginary character created by Pierre Louÿs, the poet. She told me, 'I have known over-zealous students to spend hours in the British Museum looking her up in Greek mythology.'

Whether Bilitis in *La Chevelure* is relating her experience to an intimate, or, as I prefer, soliloquizing, Mme Lotte Lehmann's suggestion in *Eighteen Song Cycles*† that, 'The first words, "*Il m'a dit*" should be sung as if with suppressed laughter' is utterly incomprehensible and misleading. The song is serious from first note to last and Debussy has written on his score *Très expressif et passionnément concentré*; the composer and poet, would turn in their graves were the song to be sung with even a hint of facetiousness; it would be tantamount to performing Wolf's *Bedeckt mich mit Blumen* with a giggle.

In *Le tombeau des Naiades* (the third Bilitis song) Mme Lehmann gets into a tangle; 'Two men are walking down the snow covered avenue' and later *mes cheveux, devant ma bouche, se fleurissant de petits glaçons* is translated as 'My beard is thick with little icicles', but one of the walkers is a girl none other in fact than Bilitis who sings, and she does not sport a beard or even the smallest of moustaches. She wears her hair 'hanging down before her mouth' not perhaps à la Mélisande but in the style known as a 'bang', or so I am informed.

With these three disparate miniatures of Wolf, Strauss and Debussy my purpose is to show, albeit briefly, the correlation between poem and pianoforte. Unsurprisingly, my exemplars are favourite songs.

* Cassell & Co., 1966.
† Cassell & Co., 1971.

Anakreon has a special niche of its own and is sublime; without love of Goethe's words and Wolf's music, its moving eloquence will not be communicated. For *Morgen* I do not claim such glory but it is justly rated as one of Strauss's loveliest songs; from it we learn the value and expressiveness of the measured silence and the iron control that this imposes. *La Chevelure*, tender and sensuous, is the most esoteric of the three, a perfect marriage of minds between singer and accompanist is necessary to do it justice.

I wrote a page or so earlier that the player *pronounces* the name of the adored *Adelaide* on his pianoforte. This is not merely a figure of speech, it is only an attempt to illustrate what should be in the pianist's heart if it is brimming over with love for the sublime music under his finger tips; he might perhaps, and with all humility, be imbued with the smallest grain of the impulse which had inspired the composer when he conceived these immortal notes.

'Music making is an act of devotion, the outpouring of a feeling which is infused with the purist, noblest essence of human love.'
(*Dr. Hans Gal. Franz Schubert and the Essence of Melody*★)

★ Victor Gollancz Ltd., 1974.

Line of Demarcation

ONCE OR TWICE I have referred on earlier pages to the solo pianist partnering the voice and it is now almost taken for granted that the virtuoso or the conductor loves playing for the singer at any opportunity.

Is there a line of demarcation?

I am reminded of a rumpus that went on in a television studio a few moments before transmission while Victoria de los Angeles and I were rehearsing. Two chaps were in violent disagreement over a matter obviously of more urgency than that which was happening on the set. We had to break off our rehearsal. Apparently the producer, Patricia Foy, from her eyrie had told the studio manager to have a vase of flowers taken away, so the studio manager seeing a man standing nearby asked him to 'kill it' (a much shorter route than the circuitous 'Please remove it from the scene'). Now this man happened to be one of the lights men but he was also a human being, he merely had to stretch out his hand and place the prescribed vase behind a screen. This he did and it started the strife, Victoria de los Angeles and I could scarcely hear one another. He had stepped over the demarcation line, he had trespassed on another man's province and the injured party—the property man—'jealous in honour, sudden and quick in quarrel'— was up in arms. History does not relate the outcome of this important matter in dispute, I only know that the two principals involved were persuaded at long last to leave the studio so that less important matters such as the preparation for Victoria's song recital could continue.

It made me realize that these men, all brothers under the umbrella of their union, are not so brotherly after all, and are much more touchy, their feelings far more easily bruised than are we supposedly aesthetic artists. The truth is a successful painter, musician, sculptor, writer, actor has to have the sensitivity of a butterfly coupled, if he hopes to survive, with the hide of a rhinoceros.

What would be the demarcation line regarding Daniel Barenboim,

the great pianist and conductor, accompanist par excellence? And
Leonard Bernstein who, to make matters worse, composes as well! Is
there no outcry from the conductors that Fischer-Dieskau stands on
the podium, baton in hand? Rostropovitch, is he not satisfied to be
hailed as the foremost 'cellist in the world? By no means, for he too
conducts and, really the limit, accompanies his wife Galina Vish-
nevskaya on the pianoforte!

The truth is, there is nothing more enjoyable than partnering a
singer in some of the glories of song literature; it is the most fascinating
and absorbing art. The study of the pianoforte score of a Wolf song
gave Artur Rubinstein infinite pleasure, he once told me. Another
Artur—Schnabel—loved playing Schubert songs for his wife Theresa
Behr-Schnabel.

I once teased Benjamin Britten for attending a Peter Pears *Liederabend* devoted to Brahms; his dislike of this composer was well known.
'Have you been converted to Brahms at last?' I asked. 'Ah', he replied
'but Clifford Curzon's playing of the accompaniments was so marvellous'. Curzon, Barenboim, Lupu, Perahia, Richter, Ashkenazy,
Brendel, Vasary, all solo pianists, have—beside their virtuosity—ultra
sensitiveness (the two virtues do not necessarily go hand in hand) and I
have heard them all accompanying singers most beautifully.

If I were to attempt to enumerate the number of *virtuosi* and conductors who love playing song accompaniments it would seem as
cosmopolitan and profuse as the list of entrants for the tennis champion-
ships at Wimbledon—including the ladies for good measure—but I
have never heard an accompanist, *pur sang*, complaining that these
famous people were poaching on his court.

Having arrogated to myself the delicate task of seeding the eight
players, I do not propose to place them in order of merit. That would
be imprudent and dangerous, but I do wish to make it clear that
Geoffrey Parsons, Karl Engel, Dalton Baldwin, Paul Ulanowsky and
many other esteemed colleagues (to say nothing of Moore with his
artful lobs from the baseline) would most certainly be seeded.

Also it will be my endeavour in another chapter to consider the
difference between instrumental sonatas in which all the artists I have
named are expert, and the playing of song accompaniments.

To put it bluntly one alludes to the soloist and *her* accompanist (but
not invariably, for Bernard Levin sent me a cartoon from some
periodical depicting a song recital, and one listener asks another 'Who
is her accomplice?') the latter being expected in the old days to provide
a shadowy background. This ukase prevailed for many years until

'What's the name of her accomplice?'

bolder spirits showed what scope, colour, poetry and responsibility resided in the pianoforte part.

Of all the great soloists, the one I have heard most frequently in partnership with Janet Baker and Dietrich Fischer-Dieskau is Daniel Barenboim. It goes without saying that with his command of the key-board he played with comparative ease Schubert's *Auf der Bruck* (On the Bruck), Wolf's *Feuerreiter* (The Fire-Rider) over which I sweated blood; but far more to the point is his deep understanding of the subtleties of these composers. His individuality, justly, is always evident without impairing in the slightest degree the perfect ensemble between voice and piano, or the corporate outlook of the partnership.

It was strange to hear Barenboim, that ebullient personality, sub-duing himself when he first appeared with Fischer-Dieskau, putting the pianoforte continually on a lower dynamic plane than the voice: with a virtuoso violinist or 'cellist he would have been on equal terms. This was only a phase and I would say now that Daniel, after much experience, is one of the finest accompanists in the world. He adores partnering Janet Baker and Fischer-Dieskau as much as I did and they most certainly enjoy him.

In case I should be misunderstood, when insisting on equal terms for voice and piano, I must make it clear I am referring to balance, weight of tone. As I have written elsewhere '. . . the greater burden of responsibility falls on the singer; it is he who *presents* the song, who marries the word with the music . . .'* and I have never lost sight of this vital fact. Conductors *qua* conductors will have none of this; listening to them accompanying a singer on the pianoforte I have sometimes wondered if they so much as listen to the voice, for they will romp and slap about like babies in the bathtub.

It can be understood that a singer—even of the eminence of Elisabeth Schwarzkopf—feels flattered when a conductor of Dr. Wilhelm Furtwängler's stature asks if he may play her *Liederabend* at the Salzburg Festival. Dr. Furtwängler alluded to it as 'my recital' and accompanied this lovely singer with the pianoforte lid fully open and, so I was told, was altogether too heavy-handed for the voice.

Dr. Bruno Walter accompanied our dear Kathleen Ferrier in an Usher Hall recital at the Edinburgh Festival. 'Why weren't you playing for her?' Aksel Schiotz asked me mournfully as the concert finished. Undoubtedly the presence of Walter added lustre to the occasion: moreover he had been a guide to Kathleen in her progress as an interpreter of *Lieder* and an inspiring influence in her professional life; he was rightly venerated as a great musician and conductor. His playing on this particular evening was deplorable and showed how necessary it is for the accompanist to have prepared himself by assiduous practising and to have maintained the discipline (much more difficult for a pianist than anybody) of self-listening. For example his playing of *An die Musik*, a hymn of thankfulness for the art of music, was painful. A violoncello-like bass affectionately reflects the vocal line; above it are repeated chords in the treble to be treated tenderly and smoothly and to be played, naturally, with the lightest touch to allow the bass tune to predominate: but these parenthetical chords were dabbed down by Walter as if he were beating eggs. Throughout the concert his habit—elementary and amateur—of playing one hand after the other in all his chording (did Kathleen know with which hand she should synchronize?) had old ladies in ecstasy, they sighed that 'It reminded them of old Vienna'. I become annoyed at the recollection of it, but when I expressed myself at the time to Audrey Christie she suggested that I was jealous, though I hope it was said to tease. Only on records have I

* *The Unashamed Accompanist* (Methuen, 1959).

heard the true Bruno Walter on the pianoforte, particularly in Schumann's *Dichterliebe* where his partnership with Lotte Lehmann was beautiful.

I am not jealous of Sir Georg Solti or of André Previn. These two artists are superb accompanists, though how they manage to keep in such excellent pianistic form with their orchestral rehearsals and performances is a mystery.

I conclude that like Walter Susskind and Wolfgang Sawallisch they were accomplished pianists before they became famous conductors.

I have heard Solti only once as an accompanist—but in a minute I recognized a master. He was playing for Yvonne Minton at a birthday celebration for Sir Robert Mayer. Two Wolf songs were performed— *In dem Schatten meiner Locken* (In the Shadow of My Tresses) (I have always conceived it as playfully tender in mood but Miss Minton was a shade too serious here) and *Ich hab' in Penna einen Liebste wohnen* (I Have a Sweetheart in Penna), brilliantly sung, and immaculately played by Solti. If I mistake not he was playing the last named in E flat—a much more difficult key than the original F—and it was thrown off with such tremendous panache that one wanted to stand up and cheer.

My beloved Janet Baker told me that André Previn asked if he might play for her at her Los Angeles recital some months ago and to quote her 'He was an inspiration'. I know André as a splendid pianist having heard him in concertos, but never as accompanist. When does he find time to practise?

I repeat I have never heard a murmur of protest from any of my fellow practitioners that superb musicians, such as I have mentioned, were trespassing on our preserves. Rather I would say they bring distinction to the art of accompaniment: by their evident love of it they exemplify its radiance and significance.

The mere fact that a famous personality, normally associated with a different sphere of music, seats himself at the keyboard attracts attention and someone in the audience will notice the piano part *for the first time* and will exclaim 'What wonderful accompaniments!'

It is only fair to add that this Philistine no matter how magnificently inept the playing, will still say 'What wonderful accompaniments!'

Dame Janet

ON SUNDAY, January 1, 1976 we had a telephone call from Janet and Keith to say 'Au revoir', they were flying to America the next morning. 'You will see something in the papers to-morrow that, I hope, will give you pleasure'. 'Janet,' I said, 'you are in the Honours list, and you are to become a Dame.' For some time we had felt that one of the world's supreme singers was deserving of this accolade and it was not an inspired piece of guess-work on my part. We said, 'Good-bye, Miss Baker; we shall never call you Miss Baker again'.

We were privileged to join our friends Janet and Keith Shelley, her husband, at luncheon on their return from Buckingham Palace on February 17. This party was carefully arranged. When Janet was appointed Commander of the British Empire (C.B.E.) some years previously the customary invitation for two, to witness the ceremony was sent to Keith. Who should go with him, Mr. or Mrs. Baker? They tossed a coin and the mother won. Now in 1976 it was the father's turn and he accordingly drove off to the Palace with Keith and the heroine, who was about to be decorated for the second time. Enid and I drove over to pick up Mrs. Baker at Janet's house and popped in for ten minutes for a cup of coffee. We returned to the car, three happy people, tingling with excitement and pride—I turned the ignition key and our merry chatter ceased. We were silent and so was the engine of the car. How can I describe that sinking feeling at the pit of the stomach which we have all experienced when nothing happens; when your self-starter makes no impression on the hitherto well-behaved smooth running machinery? You turn the key to off—and then you say to yourself, 'I will pretend I do not want the engine to start, I will take the sullen brute by surprise' and then—without giving any warning or by your leave you turn the key violently. No good. The silence was even more profound. It was broken. first by Enid giving me all sorts of advice (I loved that) and then by the quiet voice of Janet's mother with 'Well, what is to be, is to be'. (This remark impinged itself on my subconscious—never to be forgotten—for reasons I shall try to explain later—but please excuse me from delving into it at this moment, I am too worried about my confounded car.) It was then that a delivery man drove along and I asked him if he could help me: I opened the bonnet (it is the only thing I can do to a car beyond driving it) and the Good Samaritan looked very wise and told me a lot of obscure things about batteries and dynamos which he did not believe any more than I did. At length Enid took the driving seat and the Good Samaritan and I pushed, and lo and behold the engine started. We held our breaths the entire journey from Harrow-on-the-Hill to the Connaught Hotel, Grosvenor Square, for fear the engine would stall again. But it did *not* stall nor has it *ever* stalled since.

Seven of us sat down to lunch, Emmie Tillett making up the party. To be asked to join them in such a celebration, to bathe in the reflected glory of one who was so dear to us made us feel that Janet and Keith, yes and May and Bob Baker, regarded us as members of the family.

We first saw Janet in 1959 when she was singing under the baton of John Barbirolli at the King's Lynn Festival. Enid and I, in the front pew at St. Nicholas Church, exchanged glances and smiles with her. We recognized one another but did not meet till later.

Did I realize when I first heard her that I was listening to an artist destined for greatness? A leading question. It is easy to be wise after the event by saying it was obvious to me but it would not be strictly true. That I was impressed would be nearer the mark, and I would have said Janet was a young singer with a lovely voice, refined musicianship and with a serious approach. My first engagement with her came soon after this King's Lynn meeting and I recognized then what an outstanding singer this young lady promised to be. It was at the Town Hall, Middlesbrough, and we met there for our final rehearsal. Her father told me years later that he returned to the hall after parking the car to see how we were getting on: 'You were both laughing so I knew all was well'.

But it was in 1961 when we started rehearsals for her Wigmore Hall début that I began to feel that quickening of the pulse, that instinctive reaction a musician experiences, when a hidden force is suddenly communicated and to which he immediately responds. 'The quick fire leaps and instantly they understand.' Over sixty years as a professional, I have experienced this thrill only when working with the very finest musical minds and accomplished artists—and now—a final name— Janet Baker to add to the small list whom I name 'my beloveds'.

I have no newspaper criticisms of this first London recital and, with respect, what the critics wrote is of little import in the light of the triumphs the future had in store.

It must have been about this time that rehearsing in Berlin, Fischer-Dieskau asked me, 'Have you had any specially interesting recitals lately?' Without hesitation I replied, 'I have been playing for Janet Baker.' But Dieter had to admit he had never heard of her. To my astonishment the next day he exploded, 'Janet Baker is wonderful!' This insatiable man was curious to hear the singer who roused my enthusiasm and had tuned in to some broadcast concert from England. 'It was a bad orchestra, an inconsiderate conductor, but this Janet Baker sailed along serenely and undisturbed. I was deeply impressed and I want to sing with her.' And sing with her he did on many happy occasions for them both and for me.

Janet told me it was stirring for her in their duets; each seemed to know in advance what the other was going to do—how a phrase was going to be shaped—the dynamic range and extent of a nuance. 'It pleased me that my mind *in a lesser way* moved on a parallel line with Fischer-Dieskau'. These are her words, the italics are mine for they illustrate how modest she is and how great her admiration for Fischer-Dieskau.

Referring to a singer of the past Martin Cooper wrote, 'Singing was more important to her than music . . . she was greater as a singer than as an interpreter'. Knowing the singer Mr. Cooper was alluding to I am in accord: but in turn I can say of many singers for whom I have played—paraphrasing Mr. Cooper's words—'Music was more important to this artist than singing . . . he or she was greater as an interpreter than as a singer'. None of these precepts is applicable to Janet Baker, for though her voice is controlled by a virtuoso technique, though it has a natural quality of chaste voluptuousness, it is the message of the composer, the meaning of the music this voice conveys, that is always uppermost in her mind when she is singing.

In an attempt to describe the scope of her vocal colour I am choosing two widely disparate songs from her repertoire. First Stanford's setting of *La Belle Dame sans Merci* (Keats).

When she sings

> Oh what can ail thee Knight at Arms
> Alone and palely loitering;

the tone is grey and, to use a violinist's term, *senza vibrato*, so that you believe in the withered sedge, the songless birds, the fast-fading rose. It is, in a word, lifeless.

But, without any increase of tone the voice can be infused with life and warmth: the words

> She look'd at me as she did love,
> And made sweet moan,

are made melting in their allure, colourless no more, but tingling with tender desire.

The frightening contrast, harsh and cruel

> I saw their starv'd lips in the gloom
> With horrid warning gapèd wide,

is attacked with force and fury such as make the listener doubt if it is the same woman who but a few moments earlier made so seductive an appeal.

Ernest Newman said of Elena Gerhardt that one could sense by a single unaccompanied tone from her whether she was singing in the major or in the minor mode. As an old associate of Elena I would say this is an exaggeration and would rather suggest that the quality of sound she produced was prompted by the meaning of the words but *influenced* by the pianoforte harmony. And with Janet Baker the desolate bare-boned accompaniment to which she listens with concentration helps her create the colour or (as we have seen in the minor opening of the Stanford song) lack of colour she is able to command. The harmony is the root from which this response springs.

Let us see how this mastery is brought into play in my second choice. This and the Stanford song are antipodes. Where the first was melodramatic giving the singer thereby a richer palette, my Franz Schubert is an exquisite miniature.

Schöne Welt, wo bist du? (Beauteous World, Where Art Thou?). It is a stanza from an ode in honour of the Greek gods by Schiller, and sighs for the magic land, the golden age gone beyond recall. ('Times past can never never come again' sang Purcell, but Schubert expressed the same sentiment infinitely more poignantly.) Minor and major modes continually alternate: the plaintive minor—despair; the major, a furtive gleam of sunshine—consolation unattainable.

Whereas *La Belle Dame* ranged dynamically from *pp* up to *ff* we are now working more restrictively from *pp* up to *p*. (There are admittedly two bars marked *forte* which come twice, but they are only *comparatively forte*.) The shadow of despair in this song is always heard in the minor and it is only here that the voice rises above the quiet which is its norm. *Wo bist du?* is the apex of the curving vocal line and Janet gives an emphasis on the '*b*' of *bist* so that desperation is conveyed without increasing the tone disproportionately. There is no *crescendo* marked up to this *forte* but Janet prepares us by making one—and rightly so, for to sing *schöne pp* (as marked) and then to startle us with a suddenly loud '*Welt*' would be without taste and feeling. (Why did not Schubert give the instruction *crescendo*? Because he expected his interpreters to show a little imagination—he died when he was thirty-one and had little time to spare.) Her voice has the *minor* nature—which Newman felt in Gerhardt.

'Come back to us, golden age, enchanted land of song.'

Here hope is expressed in the gleaming major key and, typically Schubertian, is sung softly as if reluctant to reveal its evanescence.

This is one of those songs that speaks for itself. Janet and I, when rehearsing, did not have to discuss it, Schubert has put it there. In other words, it does not demand esoteric penetration and is none the less lovely for that, but it does need perfect vocal control with its long smooth lines, its delicate *melisma*, its occasional prepositions pitched on the high point of a phrase (*der* for instance at in *dem Feenland der Lieder*) which Janet Baker glides over so affectionately and unostentatiously as to make one grateful for Schubert's scorn of making his music tailor-made to fit verbal metre. The final *wo bist du, wo bist du?* having previously been heard twice in a despairing *forte*, is now *pianissimo*, disappearing forlornly as the song ends. We are not aware when listening to this singer that these are technical problems—she has forgotten that they exist—she believes in and is absorbed by the beauty.

In tackling an operatic role or a song, it is her instinct that is going to carry Janet Baker through, and while carefully and modestly valuing advice she does not bind herself to accept it unless it complies with a deep inner feeling. 'I feel totally at home in the theatre, a fish in water. I am not acting. The part takes possession of me, it is real not make-believe. I have had some good and helpful producers and I stand here when told, I walk there when told, but I have never been taught to act.'

In Monteverdi's *Il ritorna d'Ulisse* she sat, the picture of misery—

Penelope desolated by the prolonged absence of her husband—with arms tightly crossed, with hands clutching shoulders she made her body shrink before our eyes. We asked her who inspired her to adopt this distraught and emotive posture: she answered with one word 'Monteverdi'.

This role is one of her three favourites. She loves it for the nobility which is Penelope's, for her faithfulness to her husband and for the spirituality which is the quintessence of the woman.

Maria Stuarda of Donizetti has its special appeal because—to use her words—'of its vocal splendour'; and she believes it is the only opera in which she has had a confrontation with another woman such as she has here with Queen Elizabeth.

Having heard, thankfully several times, Janet's performance of *Les Nuits d'été* (a cycle which I have performed with fine singers over the past few decades)—I say without hesitation that she is unrivalled in this set of songs. It is no surprise therefore that Dido in *Les Troyens* is another of her favourite parts. She is a devotee of Berlioz and finds his Dido one of the finest of all mezzo roles and though she enjoys Purcell's Dido it lacks, for her, the dramatic and all-embracing quality of Berlioz.

'I am not acting, the part takes possession of me.' Never was an assertion more truly evinced than in the opera *Owen Wingrave* which was specially written for television by Benjamin Britten.

I give the briefest synopsis of the plot.

Owen Wingrave—the last of the Wingrave line—reared from infancy to be a soldier, tells the head of his military cramming establishment, Spencer Coyle, that he cannot go through with it, has no ambition to be a fighting man. All the Wingraves have been soldiers and the violent grandfather General Sir Philip Wingrave, when Owen tells him of his decision, disowns him and calls him 'Traitor. Disgrace to the family'. But the cruellest voice of all the Wingrave entourage is that of Kate Julian, Owen's betrothed. 'Coward,' she shrills and dares him to spend the night alone in the haunted room of the old house: Owen is locked in by Kate herself and found dead there a few hours later.

Many of Janet's friends were in the cast: Benjamin Luxon (Owen), Heather Harper (Mrs. Coyle), John Shirley-Quirk (Coyle), Jennifer Vyvyan (Mrs. Julian) and Peter Pears (the General).

Benjamin Britten particularly wanted the malignant Kate Julian to be played by Janet, convinced that no other singer could act the part; he told her twelve months before the opera was put into production that the part would cause her anguish—and how well he understood her. 'In rehearsal I watched the scene where Mrs. Coyle was telling Coyle what a terrible creature I was—and to hear my dear friend Heather Harper, who is so generous and so fair, saying these things hurt me—Ben saw my pain, knew what was going through my mind and came over to me, put his arm around me and consoled me.' John Amis, after the performance, asked her, 'Are you like this in real life?' No doubt it was meant as a joke but it was not the most tactful of compliments. Does John ask Tito Gobbi after his Scarpia or Iago the same sort of question?

I well remember Lilian Braithwaite, one of our finest actresses, playing a possessive mother in a play called *The Silver Cord*. She succeeded in breaking up the marriages of her sons. When she took a curtain after the last act, two women next to us started hissing her and I turned on them, 'But surely you must applaud wonderful acting!' 'She is an evil woman' was the answer. I told Lilian Braithwaite about this some months later and she said that during the play's run she had received several threatening letters. I hope my dear Janet did not suffer in this way after her marvellous portrayal of Kate in *Owen Wingrave*, for the part indeed does take possession of her.

Peter Heyworth once wrote, 'As a dramatic conception this Lady Macbeth could be imposed on a dozen operatic roles, to equally good effect'. He was referring to another singer, I hasten to add, and would never have said this about Janet Baker, for she is a different character with every role she plays. This oneness with the role spills over in a generous fellow-feeling for her associates by a sympathetic—I would say—affectionate understanding for, and response to the issues that confront them; and paradoxically is born out by her distress on listening to Heather Harper (in her role of Mrs Coyle) justly expressing her disgust of Janet (in her role of Kate).

Nobody is more aware of the moment in opera when another should have the full attention of the listener, and while her colleague holds the floor she will stand, if the circumstance warrants it, still as a statue with her back to the audience so as not to attract attention away from the singer. It is an example of artistic and unselfish consideration. Mind you, it would not have suited Feodor Ivanovitch Chaliapin. One's eyes were drawn to him as to a magnet; there might be two or more principals on the stage and a chorus of sixty all singing their hearts out but one only saw Chaliapin. In the Polovtsian Dances in *Prince Igor*, the scene packed with chorus and dancers, most of the audience looked only at Khan Kontchak even though he was enthroned on one side, to give the ballet centre stage. I know because I too was magnetized, and watching him, hugged myself with delight. Every moment I have seen and heard this majestic giant on stage I recall with relish—but he could not do what Baker can do: do nothing, and do nothing with grace and dignity.

She radiates, as Paul Jennings puts it, a luminous calm. And this brings me back to the philosophical stoicism of Janet's mother on the momentous occasion—she was agog to celebrate her daughter's accolade—when accepting the fact that my imbecile car would not budge, with 'Well, what is to be, is to be'. Perhaps Janet's 'luminous calm' is inherited; perhaps also it comes from the Christian faith which is strong in her.

The Bible gives her spiritual stimulation: in fact when presenting the annual awards to the students at the Royal Academy of Music, her address (which the Principal, Sir Anthony Lewis, told me was eloquent and delivered without any notes) was largely devoted to the parable of the talents (St. Matthew). Surely a propitious theme for such an occasion; a caution to young people not to squander but to nurture by hard work the gift that God has given them.

She herself is a shining example of humility for she is aware—how could she help it?—that she has a good voice 'But', these are her words, 'I owe it to no cleverness of my own so I have no reason to be conceited.' Dame Janet practises what she preaches—she is a hard worker, does not spare herself, studies unceasingly with concentration and fixity of purpose. Her remarkable facility for memorizing is perhaps not so facile as it seems but rather the result of patient and persistent industry.

One aspect of her individual approach to her work is her habit of ringing the changes on her pianistic partners. In nine cases out of ten, soloists of eminence prefer to work permanently with one accompanist, but Janet Baker's opinion is that all artists no matter how good they are have blanks in their musical make-up. The best of them are floored in one department or another, a stricture that does not apply to Geoffrey Parsons, but Janet enjoys collaborating with a fresh mind especially on a recital programme she has previously performed. It is a counter-action against staleness. Similarly she finds inspiration in working with different conductors. Naturally on a foreign tour she has the same partner throughout to save herself from anxiety and hurried rehearsing.

If I have given the impression that Dame Janet is a solemn person I should be sorry. She and Keith have an infectious love of life and we have had many joyous times together. From the pinnacle of my advanced age I enjoy teasing this delightful and lovable pair and since they are able invariably to give me a Roland for an Oliver I feel rejuvenated and complimented.

Her friends are mostly musicians—Daniel and Jacqueline Barenboim, Neville and Molly Marriner, Heather Harper, Raymond Leppard. But I should be abusing our friendship if I drew aside the veil of Janet's and Keith's private lives. Every celebrity has two lives, that which the general public see, hear and are at liberty to criticize if they are so disposed and which the media can commend or censure. Then there is that life which is their own and which is resolutely protected when they close their door. The publicity sought by the ubiquitous television camera for a glimpse of the star's home life with adoring family and marvelling friends grouped round her, is not to Janet's taste. She is a private person.

Janet does not travel the world in solitary splendour—there is no 'loneliness of the long-distance runner' for her. Keith is always at her side, a constant support, who relieves the artist of mundane worries. All enquiries concerning concert, operatic or recording engagements pass through his hands. Does the press want an interview? Keith considers it. Janet is escorted from home to airport, to hotel, to rehearsal, to performance without having to bother her head about passports, visas, tickets, time-tables, cars; her only care is her music and Keith's only care is Janet. They are a duo.

Even this fine man was abashed when, bound for U.S.A. they were ushered, somewhat against their will, into the VIP lounge at London Airport—coffee, magazines to hand—and 'sit here peacefully away from the crowd: we will inform you when your New York flight is called'. This courteous young official reappeared after a lapse of forty-five minutes and on Keith's quiet enquiry for news of their flight a dull thud was heard—it was the young man's jaw dropping. With glazed eyes he stammered 'Oh, it's—it's gone'. Even Keith was helpless.

I attempted in *Am I too Loud?* to pay a tribute to my wife by saying, 'In my own home I am a person of consequence. Everything revolves around me—or is made to appear to do so by one who is the most perfect of all accompanists'. To Keith Shelley I would pay a similar compliment. He is a fitting and worthy consort to a great and beloved singer.

Choose Your Partners

DAME JANET'S aversion to tying herself to one accompanist is in line with her inquiring mind and her eagerness to embrace, or at least test, new ideas. This perhaps is the secret of the freshness of her approach to all she does. Every performance is a first performance. We see a similar trend pursued by Dietrich Fischer-Dieskau. I would say that the number of pianists who have accompanied him over the past decade would easily add up to a score, and of necessity, they would all be first class.

There are, however, many singers and accompanists who have always worked together, immediately the names Peter Pears and Benjamin Britten spring to mind. Gerhard Hüsch sang with Hans Udo Müller (their art can be appreciated on records), Karl Erb's name was linked with Michael Raucheisen, until Erb's wife divorced him and ran off with Raucheisen and later married him. (Erb's response to commiseration on the loss of his wife was invariably: 'Much worse. I have lost my accompanist') Richard Tauber with the likeable Percy Kahn, who was also a talented song writer and wrote an *Ave Maria* recorded by Caruso, which was popular in America and could well have earned him high marks in an Eurovision Song Contest. Kahn strained himself unnecessarily when endeavouring to set *Du bist wie eine Blume*, a setting which was heard, alas, by Richard Capell who suggested that it only remained for Kahn to set *Der Doppelgänger* (The Shadow Double).

Gérard Souzay and Dalton Baldwin have been paired for years, as were Pierre Bernac and the late Francis Poulenc, (I still challenge anybody to tell me of a fine song writer who is *not* a good pianist) there were Marian Anderson and Franz Rupp; Kirsten Flagstad and her loyal friend Edwin McArthur; Irmgard Seefried and Erik Werba.

Going back to the days of my youth there were Gervase Elwes (rival of John Coates) and Frederick Kiddle, Harry Plunket-Greene and Samuel Liddle. Plunket-Greene had the most attractive personality, tall and slender with white hair and moustache, elegant and manly, and I wished he were my father. It took some time to 'tune in' to his singing but when at last I succeeded I derived much pleasure. Truth to tell he was one of those voiceless wonders who evoked from his many admirers the tiresome cliché 'No voice, but *what* an artist', as much as to say quality of voice was of small account. I took Mischa Léon, a tenor who was enjoying a vogue in London to a Plunket-Greene recital in Harold Craxton's studio and Léon seemed to relish the artist as much as I, for we exchanged smiles of enjoyment from time to time. It was only as we left the house and strolled down Grove End Road that Léon, looking round to see if we were beyond earshot of other members of the party, whispered to me, 'Never tell me again that that man is a singer.'

The only permanent partnership I ever made was in a pianoforte quartet with Albert Sammons violin, Lionel Tertis viola, and Cedric Sharp violoncello; for the personnel of such an ensemble, like a string quartet, must remain changeless. Again for radio work, the British Broadcasting Corporation rightly insisted on a set partnership for chamber music and I was paired with Albert Sammons (England's foremost violinist) in violin and piano sonatas, a partnership which continued on the air for many years. Later I joined Ida Haendel whom I regard as one of the great players, with a tone and ease of execution almost unrivalled.

The nearest I came to exclusivity with a soloist was my association with John Coates in the 1920s. He was the finest and most imaginative of tenors, the Peter Pears of his day. He took it for granted, although there was no written agreement between us, that I was available for all his engagements. Coates gave four or five London Recitals every season and his programmes were catholic in their taste, ranging over the fields of German, French and English song. The numerous rehearsals Coates insisted on and my own private practising for these took up most of my time. Though the Chelsea Potter—as he enjoyed calling himself—could not play one note on the piano, he taught me to accompany—no, more than that, he taught me to use my imagination. This partnership lasted for several years and established me.

Janet Baker's feeling that a different conductor or accompanist may bring a new conception to a familiar work is well understood and applauded by me, but a young accompanist needs some courage before adopting this independent attitude. His musical ambition and his pecuniary interests are aroused if a first class soloist, with ten times the accompanist's notoriety and artistry proposes a permanent working alliance. He will certainly learn a great deal, will be earning a living, and building a reputation. What are the disadvantages? His repertoire, his outlook, the quality of his pianism may well be confined if the association is protracted. My advice to a young accompanist who gets the chance to link up with an established soloist is to accept—but not to remain tied for too long.

The above paragraph, I emphasize, is directed at the *young* accompanist. It was in my formative years that I came under the spell of John Coates and was modelled on his lines. The man awakened me.

I eventually took the step of declaring myself a free-lance because it seemed necessary to play with the strings and widen my view. This linking up with so varied an assortment of players and singers broadened my outlook considerably and I cannot help wondering if my growth would have been stunted had I confined myself to working exclusively with one artist even though I held him in reverence.

Only in the last few years of my active career, when electing to work more and more with singers than with instrumentalists, has my name been linked constantly with Elisabeth Schwarzkopf, Victoria de los Angeles and Dietrich Fischer-Dieskau. It is to me a source of infinite regret that I did not have a much longer association with Janet Baker— but it was a case of bad timing on the part of her parents and mine. A letter I received from her in the early days of my retirement expresses this eloquently:

> If you only knew how often I have wished to pick up the telephone and ask you to break your retirement to do a recital with me! It is particularly heart-breaking for me to know that we can never have long years of wonderful partnership such as those you have had with three other singers I could mention; we are British musicians and it would have been such a source of pride to our profession.
>
> Your devoted
Janet

I cherish this message from a great singer whose art proves again and again that heart and depth of feeling are held in control by an active imagination and an altogether exceptional musical intelligence and taste.

It was as a mature musician that my partnership with the 'three other singers' began. This is not to say that I had nothing to learn from them (has any musician *ever* arrived at that dismal state? If he has, so much the worse for him) but each of them inspired me in their separate worlds. I had played Wolf songs long before I met Elisabeth but she brought a new bloom to them—not only by reason of her deep sympathy with Wolf's style (she loves him more than any other writer) but because I had never played them for an artist with such an incomparable technique and range of expression. As for the songs of Granados, de Falla and the modern Spaniards, who could rival Victoria? I revelled in their rich colour, in their fire, in their languid voluptuousness.

Since my early days with Coates I have played more constantly with Fischer-Dieskau than with any other artist. J. W. Lambert, when reviewing some of our records always alluded, to my delight, to 'The Great Partnership'. Not only have I had more concerts with him but without a shadow of doubt our recorded output has been vast—including well over four hundred Schubert songs not reckoning our several recordings of the three glorious cycles *Die Schöne Müllerin* (Maid of the Mill), *Winterreise* (Winter Journey) and *Schwanengesang* (Swan Song). It was a revelation to work with this man and it seemed to me that with him I went deeper into Schubert's heart and mind than ever before. Of course we covered the vast field of German Song (and for good measure Purcell and Fauré) but I stress Franz Schubert above all as he is my deep love.

When I wrote to Dieter of my intention to withdraw from public performance the following letter almost made me change my mind:

> My dear friends, Gerald and Enid,
>
> I know—or at least I think I know how difficult it was for you to write that last letter and although it made me almost cry and long to see you both soon again, I only can understand you.
>
> Gerald, working with you was the *centre* of all my doings in the singing part of my life. And if there is something like a heaven we certainly shall continue to do our job there. Our association is for life and death, 'An Unfinished Symphony'.

In 1975 my *Schubert Song Cycles*★ was published. It was dedicated to two Great Schubertians—the late Richard Capell and Dietrich Fischer-Dieskau and I had not warned Dieter of this at all—

A big surprise just arrived, your book with its dear dedication

★ Hamish Hamilton, 1975.

moved me to tears and so many happy memories come to my mind when we deeply sunk into the Schubertian world and achieved some extraordinary results one might say. I take this book with me on tour and will have the greatest pleasure to reflect in my mind what we have done together. Thank you from the bottom of my heart.

The most constant joy and most rewarding partnership of my career . . ., it was working *with you* dear Gerald, and this is reason enough to be grateful for the rest of my life.

Your friend
Dieter

Recording, 1922–1975

'THE READER has a right to know whither I am leading him,' I wrote earlier: a promise to pursue three streams of activity which for some years have dominated my life. To take recording first I must beg leave in this page to go back some fifty years in an attempt to show the powerful influence it has had on my work.

I first started recording in 1922 for His Master's Voice, this was long before the days of the microphone (the word stereo had never been heard of—at least by me), and I have been on good terms with the company ever since.

On entering the portals of the factory when I first visited Hayes, I walked between an avenue of portraits of artists who were designated, as I afterwards learned, as 'Red Label' artists: Dame Nellie Melba, Luisa Tetrazzini, Enrico Caruso, Feodor Chaliapin, Fritz Kreisler, Sir Edward Elgar and the like. I trembled a little but passed through. At this time I was looked on as an interloper for there was a kind of resident 'house accompanist'. Peter Dawson, the baritone, and one of the most popular singers of ballads in the country, told the company that he wanted me and none other to record his accompaniments. Although he was a 'Plum Label' artist (a slightly less exalted category) his records sold by the million and in consequence no objection to his condition was made.

Gradually I recorded with more and more singers and string players at Hayes and later in the company's studio in St. John's Wood, London. My early days of recording I have described in some detail in *Am I too Loud?* but I must emphasize that the haphazard hit or miss method of recording in those days seems staggering to us now. A rehearsal one or two days before a gramophone session was unheard of. Unheard of, too, was the producer. Today no record is attempted without a liaison between studio and control room; a musician who can listen quietly, dispassionately and critically to the artists, can understand what they are striving for, and is able to use the technical jargon of the recording engineers.

When war broke out in 1939 I was offered a five-year retaining fee, conditional on my recording only for H.M.V. and Columbia, now merged under the umbrella of Electrical Musical Industries. When hostilities ceased in 1945 my contract, with improved terms, was renewed: on my own stipulation these were two-year agreements and no longer, so that I was able biennially to negotiate 'improved' terms with monotonous regularity.

We often wondered whether this exclusivity was wise, for time and again I had to refuse offers from other firms wanting me to play for artists with whom I should gladly have been teamed. Yet I do not regret it in retrospect, for I would say, without exaggeration, that E.M.I. gave me more *réclame* (I prefer that term to publicity) than any accompanist had ever enjoyed before. Never previously had the accompanist's name been seen on the record, used in advertising, appeared in the reviews. The effect of this was transparent after the war when playing in America and throughout Europe, I found I was not unknown. Personally gratifying to me, but of more importance was the honour it brought to the role of the accompanist.

On a different plane from these mundane considerations was the effect recording had on my playing. If no progress had been made in the gramophone industry, in other words if transmission of sound from horn to soft wax was to be irrevocable, if the hammers on the piano were inevitably to be thinned of their felt, if for the purpose of getting a good balance between violin or voice it continued to be essential for the piano to be thirty feet away from the horn, then I too would have made no progress and would now be a consummate banger. The electrical process with its ultra sensitive microphone revolutionized the artist's approach. He could now listen to himself and learn. For the first time on record he could hear the difference between *pianissimo* and *piano*, between *piano* and *mezzo piano*, he could hear the minutest dynamic rise and fall, the subtlest nuance. I was sufficiently honest with myself to be aware of my own lack of sensitivity and I found there was no excuse now for ragged ensemble.

They tell me that on record I have a distinctive tone—though here I am sceptical: they say that I am sensitive—and here I concur. Whatever qualities I have acquired I owe not only to my contact with superb artists but also to the gramophone.

My recording so far had been in England but in 1938 I had one long stay in Berlin for the Hugo Wolf Society. Walter Legge, its founder, had assembled vintage artists of that time—Martha Fuchs, Karl Erb, Herbert Janssen, Gerhard Hüsch, Helge Roswaenge.

(Berlin was a depressing city that year. One saw little boys of ten or eleven, not playing football or tennis but marching in column, grim of face, with the swastika emblem on their shirts; one saw dignified white-haired old gentlemen stretching their arms in the air like clock-work dolls as they met friends or acquaintances with 'Heil Hitler'. A pitiful loss of dignity. I admired Martha Fuchs because she refused to conform to the obligatory salute; in response to the 'Heil Hitler' from the concierge at the recording studio, she persistently replied 'Grüss Gott'. It was dangerous and it was brave. Herbert Janssen the gentlest of men was distressed by a letter, not signed 'With love from Mother' but 'From your Mother with true German greetings'.)

Ten years later Berlin was to become more and more the venue for *lieder* sessions. Still under the auspices of E.M.I.—their German wing is Electrola—I worked with Elisabeth Schwarzkopf, Elisabeth Grümmer, Victoria de los Angeles, Dietrich Fischer-Dieskau, Hans Hotter, Hermann Prey and others.

We recorded in one of Berlin's nicest suburbs, Zehlendorff (our car taking us *en route* through the beautiful Grunewald), with the late Fritz Ganss in charge of the sessions. Fritz was a large generous man with an extensive knowledge of music; it was a pleasure to work with him and we became good friends. Like all successful recording managers he had unlimited patience, tact and inexhaustible good humour.

Our sessions took place in a church hall. There were two drawbacks —each concerned with flights. We recorded as distant as it was possible to be from Tempelhof Airport, but in certain weather conditions, a flight path passed over us and often we had to break off because of plane noises. Another disadvantage was the long flight of stairs between the studio and the control room. With Dieter I never had to climb these until our session was finished, when we would go aloft and listen critically to play-backs of the evening's work and decide then and there what we should repeat. With Elisabeth, on the contrary, the pitter patter of our merry footsteps was heard continually. This was particularly trying for me in Wolf's *Italienisches Liederbuch* (Italian Songbook), as Elisabeth would take off for the attic after one minute's singing, not liking the tonal quality of the play-back below stairs.

Without impairing my cordial relations with E.M.I. I decided in the 1960s to freelance, and it was early in that decade that Deutsche Grammophon Gesellschaft asked Fischer-Dieskau and me to embark on the huge task of recording our three collections of Schubert songs in Berlin. I nearly wrote 'all Schubert's songs' but that would be inaccurate for even with his love for the composer Dieter did not aspire to such feminine songs as *Gretchen am Spinnrade* (Gretchen at Her Spinning-wheel) or the two *Suleika* songs. Elena Gerhardt frequently performed *Die Winterreise* which is of course a cycle for a man, and did it most successfully—Lotte Lehmann sang Schumann's *Dichterliebe* (Poet's Love), but there are only exceptional instances where a man's singing of a woman's song is acceptable.

The D.G.G. studio was situated in the suburb of Tempelhof and was sound proof; no flights to be heard, no flights to be climbed. It was constructed solely for recording and was far more congenial for the artists to work in than the difficult conditions that prevailed in the church hall previously described. Here at Tempelhof, contact between artists and recording manager was constant, and our relations became very friendly.

It is only fair at this juncture, that I pay tribute to the three producers who in turn played such a valuable part in making this big assignment such a success: they are Rainer Brock, Otto Gerdes and Dr. Ellen Hickman. The sound engineer from beginning to end was Hans-Peter Schweigmann. These colleagues and their assistants were never ruled by the clock; the one to cry halt would be Fischer-Dieskau at the first suspicion of tiredness in the voice.

The understanding between Dieter and me was so complete that while the tapes were running we would, with barely a word exchanged, repeat an entire song. I knew when he was dissatisfied with himself and I recognized my short-comings only too well. A song might be taped two or three times; I emphasize this because Fischer-Dieskau had a dislike for the 'patch-work quilt' method of recording, whereby the finished product is cut and taped and edited from a dozen 'takes'.

When we stopped it did not mean a cessation of work for we would sit down and listen carefully, sometimes repeatedly, to decide our plan of campaign for the morrow.

We recorded nearly 500 Schubert songs if duets with Janet Baker and quartets with her, Elly Ameling and the tenor Peter Schreier are included. Is it any wonder that Bernard Levin in *The Times* revealed the sordid truth of the matter, namely that we had abducted poor Franz Schubert and smuggled him to Berlin in order that we should be kept supplied with more and more songs? In fact there are many titles in this collection that Fischer-Dieskau and I had never performed.

Naturally a few of these unknowns were not up to the standard we have come to expect from the Master (mostly composed in his formative years), but many of them delighted us and their neglect seems astonishing.

★   ★   ★

My many recording sessions in Berlin from 1948 to 1975 were not confined to Schubert for with Elisabeth Schwarzkopf and Fischer-Dieskau practically every song Wolf wrote was put on tape, and inevitably album after album of the other great Lieder composers.

Perhaps the toughest undertaking apart from the massive Schubert story was the wish of E.M.I. to put 134 Richard Strauss songs on record: I say tough because the piano accompaniments are often prodigiously difficult. 'How did you like playing *Lied an Meinen Sohn*?' Alfred Brendel asked me with a knowing look; and in truth it is what is known in intellectual circles as a humdinger.

Still, over my half century of recording it is the Schubert albums that have given me more pleasure on the whole than any other records I have made. Pleasure yes, but not self-satisfaction; there is a difference for I am only too conscious that I should or could have done better.

So little known are many songs in this vast collection that in the latter part of this book I propose to enjoy myself by attempting to describe some of these treasures.

First Aid

PETER DAWSON, to whom I referred in the last chapter, was a most jovial man and I think he enjoyed recounting his early experiences to one a good deal his junior. Two of them I relate here; there is a moral attached to them which any aspiring professional musician should take to heart, though Peter was far too straightforward a character to preach a sermon.

As a first-rate ballad singer with a remarkably fine baritone voice he was allotted his fair share of engagements at the Henry Wood Promenade Concerts at the Queens Hall. When the 'Proms' were under the auspices of Messrs. Chappell & Co. the programmes differed widely from those of today, sponsored by the B.B.C. They were divided into two parts, the first half more serious with symphonic music and operatic arias, the second part much lighter included ballads with pianoforte accompaniment. But between these arias—comparatively early in the evening—and the ballads, there would be a symphony followed by a long intermission so that a singer had an unconscionable gap of perhaps an hour and a half between his appearances. When Charles Saunders, a tenor built on G. K. Chesterton lines, suggested to the lad Peter Dawson—experiencing his first Prom engagement—that 'we go round the corner for a drink' young Dawson was over-awed at the wonder of it. Going off for a drink with the great Charles Saunders!

The pub round the corner (it is known as the Glue Pot) was full, but Saunders, obviously known to all, stood behind the crowd and just raised two fingers in the V sign and very promptly two extremely large whiskies were in their hands. Dawson, anxious to play the man, downed his quickly in order to stand his round, 'I'll order two more, Mr. Saunders, when you have finished yours'. 'That's your drink, Dawson'—indicating his own unfinished drink—'I never take two bites at a cherry.' So Dawson drank that half glass, ordered two more, and 'when I walked on to the platform to sing my group—the hall was going up and down, I was seeing double and I have no recollection of how I sang or how I got through.'

★ ★ ★

According to Dawson the ballad concerts on Saturday nights at the Central Hall, Westminster, were so informal that there were no printed programmes, singers announced their items from the platform. I feel that the words 'Saturday night' suggested a more free and easy approach—at least they did to one singer, a tenor.

He had that 'Saturday night' feeling—he was very much the worse for wear and was more than a little unsteady on his pins: his opening offering was to be an aria from *La Reine de Saba*, a Gounod opera.

Now the walk to stage centre is a goodly stretch at the Central Hall and Peter Dawson told me that before setting out on his trek to the piano he saw our tenor eye his goal with a fixed stare as if threatening the instrument not to move. Then he set out bravely with his feet at an angle of ten minutes to two, his arms bent at elbow like stabilizers to keep balance. Arrived miraculously at the piano—he was very short—he stood in its curve facing the audience with arms stretched to left and right clutching the sturdy instrument as the blind Samson embraced the pillars in the hall of the Philistines. He waited, then taking a deep breath he forsook the buttress which Steinways had provided for him and took one step forward to announce his item. In high pitched and choking tones he cried 'Lend me your aid' and fell flat on his face.

5   Seventieth Birthday Record: Jacqueline du Pré and author

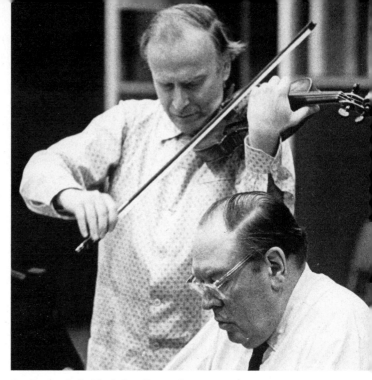

6 Seventieth Birthday Record:
above: Yehudi Menuhin and author
below: Daniel Barenboim and author

7 *above:* Rehearsing with Dietrich Fischer-Dieskau. *below:* The author explaining cricket to Régine Crespin, Yehudi Menuhin and Mstislav Rostropovitch (Paris, 1974)

8   The author

Sometimes Ashamed

'WHAT WERE the accompanist's thoughts as he played for her?' asked Ernest Newman of me after listening to a record of Mrs. Florence Foster Jenkins. This lady sang constantly one-quarter of a tone flat—it was painful to hear. 'He was thinking of his fee,' I answered.

I don't suppose there is an accompanist living who has not found himself associated in public with a partner so bad that he has felt thoroughly ashamed. Although I have had some wonderful concerts in Paris I had two experiences there which continue to haunt me; one was reading in the morning paper, 'M. Moore should have been ashamed to appear with this violinist' and I writhe when I think of the concert and when I recall that notice. Then—and it *would* happen in Paris and not long after—I played for a soprano of repute (Covent Garden, the Met, the Opéra-Comique) with a brilliant voice whose rehearsals had been pleasurable, but who turned up at the Salle Gaveau for her recital thoroughly stoned, tight, plastered, whatever you like to call it. An Amsterdam critic, after I had accompanied a third so-called singer, (recommended to me by Coenraad V. Bos of all people), wrote 'Gerald Moore could not have accepted this engagement from the highest of motives.'

'The sometimes ashamed accompanist' I could call myself. These nightmares have to be endured by a youngster. Every accompanist has had the experience in his early days of being a mercenary; it is only when he has established himself beyond question that he can afford to try to persuade the bad artists to postpone their début, until such time as they are ready.

There was no joy in playing for bad singers, but it was easy, I speak callously, because you resigned yourself to the hue and cry of life-saving.

Fortunately there are two other categories beside the bad ones; they are the good and the middling. By 'the good' I mean the super artists:

the Bakers, the Schwarzkopfs, the Fischer-Dieskaus because they are an inspiration and raise you while you are in partnership with them to their level and, in spite of high tension, your work is unadulterated pleasure.

Unfortunately super-artists are few and far between and most of the accompanist's itinerant professional life is spent at a lower altitude, in company with those who must be consigned to the middling category. These are a large package, the bulk, coming between the cream at the top and the unfortunates.

'Mr. Moore,' I am sometimes asked, 'do you remember playing for me?'

'Madame, forgive me but I do not, but let me tell you this—if you had been bad I should have remembered you.' And then under my breath I add, 'but if you had been exceptionally good I would have remembered.'

It is these, rather than the 'goodies and baddies' who are often more trying to work with; perhaps they are possessors of fine voices but have a vacuum between the ears (the secret of their resonance?), nit-wits musically or, vice versa have musical taste and imagination but poor vocal equipment, of whom we can say joining the chorus, 'No voice, but what an artist!'

The voiceless marvels can be particularly irksome because they sometimes delve into regions beyond the realms of reason. They probe, they ponder, they consult and they discuss at rehearsal before a note of music has been sounded. It is certain that were the shade of the long departed composer present at these occult scrutinies he would be astonished to learn of the hidden depths of meaning waiting to be revealed in some simple page of music that he had jotted down without any thought other than the joy of spring, the moonlight night or what have you.

Yes, let us take a moonlight night—*Mondnacht* by Schumann, one of the most exquisite nocturnes ever written. The accompanist evokes the mood, paints the picture by his playing and his 'pacing' of the six-bar introduction; it must have commas, it must take breaths and there should be no evidence at any time of the inflexible bar line. Schumann's instructions are *Zart, heimlich* (tenderly, secretly); Chopin would have added *Tempo rubato*. It is a joy to play and I cherish every single note of it. Rehearsing it with a V M (voiceless marvel) I reached the end of my prelude, but instead of singing my companion started a discussion. 'Do you know, I have never heard it played more beautifully. But I wonder if your playing is too warm; after all it is not sunlight it is moonlight and although you play it as softly as can be imagined I wonder if you could—without losing one iota of that *pianissimo* or altering one whit the shape of your phrases—I wonder if the whiteness of the moon can be suggested and the slight chill of the night air?'

To digress for a moment, Ernest Newman* tells us that in his orchestral prelude to *Hamlet* Franz Liszt instructs the trumpeter to play one long note *sehr düstre* (very gloomy). But how can the poor fellow depict Hamlet's dejection by one single note? He has played the note millions of times during his career but this special note must be blown differently from the others. Again Newman suggests that in a passage marked *ironisch*—where Hamlet is being cynical at Ophelia's expense, the only way the players can suggest they are being ironical is by winking at the audience.

Returning to my VM and *Mondnacht*, there were several alternatives open to me. I could have said 'You are talking like an idiot' (rather abrasive?) or 'You are wasting time'. Neither of these ploys can be warmly recommended if the VM and I were to remain on amicable terms: I *could* have played the introduction with my coat collar turned up (the chill of evening!); I saved my breath to cool my porridge in answer to his hyperbole by replying 'Nothing easier', and I played it exactly, as near as maybe, as I had played it before with this difference: namely, I altered my facial expression and my posture; I wore the faintest—perhaps even supercilious frown and looked aloof; I raised my eyes away from the keyboard to the north-east cornice of my studio. He said, 'That's absolutely marvellous, I am sure that is what Schumann wanted.' I said quite gently, 'Now you sing, I won't play the introduction again' (I was afraid of getting a crick in the neck) and what happened? The poor fellow sang consistently out of tune and I had to set to work in an attempt to put him right.

I can imagine someone saying 'But this maligned singer had an idea, perhaps Moore was lacking in divine afflatus.' This is possible: the accompanist should ever be ready to consider more than one point of view, but even the most critical reader will concede that in two phrases stretching over a mere six bars of the most delicate texture and of uniform *piano* it is not to be taken for granted that the time of day and temperature can be communicated. It becomes a matter of sorcery.

What is one to say if, instead of an introduction like *Mondnacht* you

---

* *Opera Nights* (Putnam, 1943).

have one single chord to play prior to the voice's entry and the composer (not the materialization of a long departed shade but the man in substance) cries 'No. I want that chord to be of an altogether different colour'? It was a simple chord marked *mezzo forte*.

This happened when Kirsten Flagstad was recording *Arie antiche* which had been arranged—most musically and acceptably—by a compatriot of hers who was acting as my page-turner. I played the chord again.

'Let me show you,' he said. I stood up and he played the chord. Then he moved over and I played the chord.

'No,' he said and played it again.

This musical chairs went on for two minutes or more and I was getting more and more angry.

All this time Flagstad stood ready to sing, waiting only till some decision had been reached over this wretched chord. It was the first song on our recording programme and I realized that at this rate we would have to take up residence in the studio; I looked up appealingly to the singer who by now had been listening to the same chord played in exactly the same way eight or more times. The situation was solved in a typically abrupt Flagstad manner with no frills; she looked at the young man and said, 'Go home.' There were no further arguments and I played the chord exactly as the unfortunate composer and I had been playing it all the time.

This is not typical of composers. Alan Rawsthorne said to Pini and me when we were playing his violoncello sonata 'Do anything you like.' Other composers, Vaughan Williams, Arthur Bliss, Poulenc, have, in my experience, interfered very little with singers and players who were doing their best to reproduce what they read on the score.

But my record (not a gramophone record but my *ne plus ultra*) where a single solitary common chord was involved was when rehearsing a Rachmaninoff song. I played the chord and sustained it not only with the pedal but with my fingers holding down the notes. I waited for my soprano to begin: after a long pause she said:

'Do you mind playing it again?'

'Not at all.' I played it—fingers and hands moveless. I waited.

She turned with a puzzled expression on her face. 'It sounds funny to me.'

'It may sound funny to you, but I am playing exactly what is written and I find no inclination to laugh.'

'Mr. Moore, do you mind once again?'

'Delighted.' Once more I played it. She was moveless. I was moveless.

She turned to me and said, 'I know what it is; you are playing too fast.'

Am I inventing this? It happened, word for word, as I have related it.

Lecture Recitals, 1942–1975

FOR SOME considerable time I had been turning over in my mind the possibility of lecturing on the art of accompaniment, being prompted quite honestly, by resentment. I felt that this branch of musical activity, to borrow Lionel Tertis's sobriquet for the viola, was the Cinderella of arts. It was painful to me, with my modest ambition, to discover in a review of a programme of violin and pianoforte sonatas or in a recital of a Schubert Song Cycle, that the pianist's name was not mentioned at all, or if his name did appear it was dragged in as an afterthought at the tail-end of the notice.

The daughter of the late Coenraad von Bos, a famous accompanist, told me over a luncheon party in Holland that I had had a good review in Amsterdam for a concert with Kathleen Ferrier; she searched in her bag and passed the clipping to me. 'You are like my father,' she said, 'he always started reading at the bottom of the notice.' Unfortunately the bottom of the notice can be docked. Once or twice a critic has said to me, 'I am sorry the compliment I paid you was clipped off by the compiler,' to which I have replied, 'A pity you put it at the bottom.'

A few weeks ago while reflecting on this chapter I received an American music magazine called *Clavier*. It had an excellent interview with one of America's top accompanists Samuel Sanders and I read to my astonishment that 'Gerald Moore, who has made accompanying an honourable profession, came to Chicago some years ago to play for Elisabeth Schwarzkopf. He arrived at the hall to rehearse but on seeing his name omitted from the billing went back to his hotel, packed his bags and returned to New York.' I wrote at once to the editor of this most reputable periodical to say that this statement was quite incorrect. To begin with, Mme Schwarzkopf was a dear friend of mine, and she, as a great artist, would have been as indignant as I over this insult to her partner. I would in no wise have deserted her and left her stranded. Here is what actually happened and I have recorded it in *Am I too Loud?*

I examined in Chicago withut most care the posters of Renata Tebaldi's recital; I read her name, the name of the hall, the name of her impresario, the time and date, the make of the pianoforte, the ticket prices. The programme was printed in detail, but no mention was made of the artist who was to partner her—one of Italy's foremost accompanists—Georgio Favoretto.

This Chicago episode occurred during one of my lecture tours in the U.S.A., but much earlier—over thirty years ago—I had decided to campaign on behalf of the accompanist and his art and to make it quite clear that I had no wish to change my role, was not one whit dissatisfied with the work I had adopted—for I loved it.

All this will be regarded by my younger reader as 'old hat', and I am glad to be able to agree with him. Thanks to the fact that the standard of accompanying in Europe and America is extremely high at the present time, thanks too, to the interest virtuoso pianists and famous conductors take in partnering singers, the public has been brought to realize how vital is the contribution made by the man at the piano. Is it egotistical of me to hope that my lecturing here, there and everywhere contributed a little to this happier state of affairs?

My first attempt at a lecture recital was made at the suggestion of Myra Hess, who had heard me talking on the radio, and she invited me to repeat it at one of her lunch hour concerts at the National Gallery. A repetition verbatim would have been complicated since my B.B.C. talk had been interspersed with records, so I compromised, and with the enthusiastic assistance of my friend Roy Henderson and his pupil Joan Taylor, I compiled a lecture to which they contributed songs and duets. It could not have been so bad, for C.E.M.A. (Council for the Encouragement of Music and the Arts, later to become the Arts Council of Great Britain) wanted to engage me for lectures throughout the country. I decided to make chamber music my subject.

A fine young 'cellist Eileen Croxford, a pupil of the late Ivor James and subsequently of Pablo Casals (she is now the wife of the pianist David Parkhouse and they formed the London Group, a first rate ensemble) consented to assist me. Included in our programme were the Brahms Sonata in E minor and Fauré's *Elégie*; these gave me opportunities to explain how many were the occasions when the 'cello had to retire into the background and accompany the piano (when the latter had the tune) and how the responsibility for getting a good balance had to be shared by the two players.

Always the pianist bears in mind that the deeper voiced 'cello can easily be outweighed by the pianoforte; by contrast the violin, with its high *tessitura* can soar above strong pianoforte tone with ease. In this instance, in my talks, I drew a parallel between the 'cello and the bass voice of Chaliapin, between the violin and the high soprano of Elisabeth Schumann. Chaliapin had a big voice but its deep tones could easily be covered by a careless pianist; on the contrary the silvery luminosity and lyrical quality of Schumann, though lacking the volume of the giant bass, carried easily over the pianoforte tone.

To demonstrate the other side of the coin I persuaded Eileen to take passages for the 'cello marked *pp* on the score, but to play them excessively loudly. This distortion of course drowned the soft tune reposing in the pianoforte, making the music grotesque and meaning-less. Though practically unheard I continued to play softly with a display of over-acted emotion which, coupled with this lop-sided balance, caused a good deal of laughter. Then I would say 'Some 'cellists, present company excepted, like to play *fortissimo* at all times'. This laughter was important for it showed that my listeners were receptive and it gave me encouragement, to change my mood to more serious considerations. The humour was the sugar-coating on the pill. If this observation makes some of my more musically erudite readers throw up their hands in horror I would remind them that I was not talking in the sheltered groves of academe but addressing, as my lectures gathered momentum, large audiences consisting for the most part of the General Public.

I wanted to vary this lecture by finding a violinist to assist me. Who could give me better advice than Bernard Shore (the metaphorical heir of Lionel Tertis) with whom I had played viola and piano sonatas so often? Bernard suggested that I ask Gertrude Collins and I certainly do not regret following his advice. One of the sonatas we played was Beethoven's Opus 24, known as the Spring Sonata. It is a delicious work, with a Scherzo as saucy as may be, with Beethovian caprice whose feature is the chase of one instrument after the other; the violin plays the same tune as the piano, lags one beat behind and never catches up.

(To illustrate this I recall a member of the congregation of my church in Toronto. His resonant voice dominated the rest of us when we recited the Lord's Prayer. He started his 'Our' after we murmurers had said 'Father' and with iron rhythmic control maintained the same pace throughout the prayer, so that his final 'Amen' was an un-accompanied solo. He never varied his tone or timing.)

To hear Beethoven's chase is to smile. I would tell the audience that as a young man I had toured with the violinist Marie Hall in South Africa, where she was a big attraction, and this Spring Sonata was on our programme. We started the tour at Cape Town and were told that the press notices on this first concert were important as they would be circulated all through the Union, as it was then called. Miss Hall and I had rehearsed diligently on the boat and gave a performance which made us fairly happy. Alas, the Olympian critic who muses under the shadow of Table Mountain complained that 'The two artists were *never together* in the Scherzo—it was obviously under-rehearsed and Moore, instead of following, was too assertive and led the way'. But this took place in 1929 and perhaps the critic during the intervening half century has learned a little about the work.

Next, Gertrude and I turned to Mozart's Sonata in E flat (K 302), it was a work I had often played with Szymon Goldberg. At rehearsal Szymon once asked me what I felt Mozart wanted in the second movement; a nice point. It is a Rondo marked *andante grazioso* and cannot be called one of those soul-stirring and ineffable inspirations that Mozart could pour out so unstintingly when in the vein. It is in 2/4 time with a subject, square in shape and formal in mood. Gertrude and I played the theme as a slow march and later played it as if it were a stately pavan. A third approach, which admittedly took the starch out of it (for both march and pavan treatment wore a stiff collar), was to find a way of imparting some fervour to it (but fervour in a controlled degree, for it was not patterned to be flushed with passion) by giving the phrases curves, with slight rises and falls, instead of one-dimensional line. We did our very best to make each procedure convincing.

The object of this Mozartian exercise was to show the difference between absolute music and programme music: how the former presented more problems to the players than music which told a story, such as opera or song. Programme music does not demand words however: the *Pastoral Symphony*, Debussy's *La Cathédrale Engloutie*, Ravel's *Pièce en forme de Habanera* speak for themselves. This is a wide subject and I did not intend to delve too deeply into it. I wanted to teach my listeners—perhaps even uplift them—in my own way, by entertaining them. My purpose was to let the music demonstrate what I had previously been talking about; yet many a listener told me he had enjoyed our music so much that he would have preferred less talking and more playing. This comment, much as I enjoyed working with Eileen and Gertrude, defeated my object, so I decided I must go it alone. How could I start? How, immediately on entry, rivet the attention, rouse the interest of some poor husband who had been dragged out braving the foggy night to listen to me?

It was then I bethought me of *Il Bacio* (The Kiss). Everybody in the world knows the tune, but do they know the accompaniment, and even if they do *not* know the accompaniment, does it matter very much? The answer is No. But the trouble is that there are vast numbers of people calling themselves musical who think the accompaniment to Schubert's *Der Lindenbaum* (The Lime Tree) or *Der Neugierige* (The Questioner) of no more significance than the Oom pah pah, Oom pah pah of Arditi's *Il Bacio*. So I would sit down with simulated concentration and do my Oom pah pahs until I began to show obvious signs of boredom—the effect of this was to start the audience tittering. When I heard these signs of amusement I would stop—turn in my seat as if I were going to speak—restrain myself—and plunge back to the keyboard grudgingly, with more Oom pah pahs: these, however, instead of plodding along in D major now made the daring(!) modulation into A major. By this time the audience was really laughing outright. This was the psychological moment to show them how enchanting some piano parts could be and how Schubert used them to illustrate a scene. *Whither?* and *Singing on the Water* with their silvery rippling were obvious choices; we moved from them to the subtleties of *The Lime Tree* with its summer breeze rustling the leaves and its wintry blast howling through the naked branches. *Der Leiermann* (The Hurdy Gurdy man) was a marvellous paradigm for displaying Schubert's unparalleled genius for translating picture and mood through the medium of the keyboard. The halting rhythm of its piano part portrays the laboured movement of the hoary player, and the drone in the accompaniment, with its repetitive bass is a speaking likeness of an old barrel organ. It is a picture of unutterable sadness and world-weariness. I referred above, with sarcasm, to Arditi's daring modulation (*Il Bacio*) from D major to A major, but Schubert in *The Hurdy Gurdy Man* does not modulate at all! Why then do musicians claim it as one of the greatest songs ever written? I partially parry the question by saying that this is the magic of Franz Schubert. Other composers do magical things but one can see so often *how* they have done it. Schubert defeats us.

The necessity for the player to understand what the singer was singing about was another subject for me. I know my friend Alec Robertson will not mind my repeating a story he tells against himself. He is now a German scholar but as a boy of seventeen he did not understand a word of the language. This did not prevent him singing in German, for a few friends, to his own accompaniment, Schumann's *Frauen-Liebe und Leben*. After the sixth song of the cycle he was rudely interrupted by a question 'Are you feeling all right?' 'Yes,' said Alec, extremely annoyed. 'I'm glad to hear it, because you have just had a baby'. The title of this cycle is *Woman's Love and Life*.

In Schubert's *Wandering* (the first song in the *Maid of the Mill*) every verse is note for note the same as the next, and the singer will vary his expression, his tempo, phrasing, dynamics to give meaning to his words. Should not the pianist treat his contribution likewise? There is no law in heaven or on earth to prevent him; but he must understand what it is all about. Schubert was sparing in the use of expression marks and performers must use some imagination.

Brahms, if and when we eventually meet, may show displeasure at my cavalier treatment of his *Vergebliches Ständchen* (Vain Serenade) for I do not obey his expression marks in this song at all. The young fellow calling up to his sweetheart's window sings lustily, without caring a cuss who hears him, and according to Brahms the maiden replies in the same lusty tone; but this is unreasonable, for in the final verse she warns the boy of the proximity of mama. It is more lifelike surely, to lighten the colour when the girl sings; there should be a suggestion of grace and femininity from singer and pianist. As for the final verse where the girl tells her lover to go home to bed, it is sung with amusement in the voice, and the accompaniment suggests a laughing girl: but this cannot be conveyed if the pianist strictly adheres to the composer's instruction, which is *legato*. I like to play it with sustaining pedal but— and here is the rub—with *staccato* touch, lightly and playfully, and it is the *staccato* that transmits the girl's laughing dismissal of the village Romeo.

This flouting of the composer's instructions, I add parenthetically, is all very well when explained in a talk where my personal interpretation of the text is being presented, but I counsel any young accompanist only to practise what I have preached with extreme care. Truth to tell I might exaggerate my *staccato* playfulness in a lecture but would underplay it in a performance with a singer; the very fact that I bore the laughter of the girl in mind, would actuate the playing.

One of my pet subjects was to illustrate how often the responsibility for evoking the poem's mood is found in the piano part, before the entry of the voice. Sometimes with Schubert it provides a précis of the story as in *Tränenregen* (Teardrops): the alternating phrases now rising in hope with a slight *crescendo*, now sinking despairingly with a corresponding *diminuendo*. 'Does she love me or does she not?' That is the question the perplexed boy is asking himself. The answer is given in the piano postlude when the dying fall sinks despondently into the negative minor.

Earlier in the same cycle (*Die Schöne Müllerin*) comes my beloved *Der Neugierige* (The Questioner). How could a question possibly be more realistically expressed in musical terms than in the piano introduction?

I enjoyed, too, playing the four bar prelude to *Frühlingstraum* (Dream of Spring) from the *Winter Journey* cycle with the little hint Schubert throws out—albeit imperceptibly—that spring has come. (If the reader looks at the score he will find a cuckoo call in the fourth bar—though it should not be given any emphasis at all. Schubert himself was perhaps unconscious of its existence.) My audiences in England were intrigued when I told them that this fancy of mine fell flat in America: with good reason, for this harbinger of spring is not known on the other side of the Atlantic.

In an earlier chapter referring to *La Chevelure* (Debussy) I wrote that the pianoforte's introductory passage must be played 'Not too strictly in tempo' and I recommended that 'time must be allowed' here and there. I remember vividly Peter Pears addressing a gathering of musicians and pleading passionately for more *rubato* in their performances. He and Benjamin Britten felt exactly as Fischer-Dieskau and I over its importance.

Rubato was a fruitful subject. I showed how certain pieces of music if sung or played in strict time, with rigid machine-like precision maintained from bar line to bar line, would lose all meaning: feeling, poetry, grace would be stamped out of them. I played a Nocturne of Chopin with unyielding exactitude of tempo (not the entire piece; it would have been intolerable) and I did my best with it, but it was impossible to infuse eloquence or meaning into it. By contrast I played the same page or so over again but this time using *rubato*, playing with flexibility, 'taking my time' with rhetorical pauses, with a space between phrases for a breath. I emphasized that elasticity of rhythm is not confined to lyrical and *cantabile* music, heroic music needs it also. The use of *rubato* in Chopin's A flat Polonaise, for example, gives muscle to the music. A great virtuoso's rhythmic control is simple evidence that he is master of *rubato*: this was the secret of Fritz Kreisler's magic and can be enjoyed on so many of his records.

I remember listening with Elisabeth Schwarzkopf and Walter Legge to a scale passage on a Kreisler record, *Caprice Viennois*. It was executed with such marvellous grace, such elegant freedom from uniformity that we went crazy over it and played the same passage over and over again.

The act of demonstrating *rubato* tempts one to exaggerate when illustrating and I said as much to my listeners. It is a subtle affair. *Rubato* literally means 'robbed', not 'borrowed', and it is a fallacy to believe that stolen time has to be repaid, that after slowing up, compensation is made by hastening. Never returning what he takes, the thief has one desire in common with the musician's *rubato*—namely—the avoidance of detection.

'I have played for many singers . . . over the last half century and while I was sometimes criticized on one count or another, I was never condemned for my love of elasticity or flexibility; nor did I ever find myself at odds with my partner. The bar line is not made of iron and the singer should not be imprisoned by it. Because of the over-riding importance of the phrase, one bar (or measure) can take more time than another, perhaps because it holds the high point in the phrase, a high point (not necessarily the topmost note) by reason of a subtle turn in the melody or because of a vital word or poignant change of harmony in the accompaniment, and its significance can be registered gently and persuasively or driven home with force as the occasion requires.'*

I did not insist that *rubato* must be used at all cost every time the singer opened his mouth. The rippling *Wohin?* (Whither?), the impetuous *Mein* (Mine) or, to go to the opposite extreme, the slow moving *Litanei* can be sung in strict time, and indeed it would be indefensible to distort them, but a sensitive singer listening to his own recording even in these songs might be surprised to find how often he deviates—minutely—from the ticking metronome. The point is that the divergence is so slight that it is acceptable and unnoticed.

Yet I suggested that there are songs which if performed *without* *rubato* would be distressing: a dozen spring to my mind at once in this category:

Nacht und Träume (Night and Dreams: Schubert). I would like to know of a singer who does *not* want to give just a very little more time to the three quavers on 'du sinkest' in his second bar. I would dare any pianist to play in strict time that sublime moment when the music moving gently in B major falls with unbelievable tenderness into the arms of G major. Yes, it must be allowed a little time to settle.

---

* *The Schubert Song Cycles* (Hamish Hamilton, 1975).

Nähe des Geliebten (Nearness of the Beloved). A strophic four-verse song in which Schubert's divine melody goes for nothing, is shorn of beauty, if it is starched and ironed into pleats.

Mondnacht (Schumann's Moonlit Night). The singer gives his semi-quaver figure leisure. The accompaniment is punctuated with commas, periods and paragraphs. Ethereal repeated notes are pliant and not played with monotonous regularity.

Ich Grolle Nicht (I'll Not Complain: Schumann). Even the iron in the soul of the poet must not make the music iron bound. The repeated chords, as in the tender *Mondnacht* though now sinewy, must be pliable. As for 'auch brieht' in the third bar, the singer telling us his heart is broken will not want to gloss over these vital words in slavish adherence to the metronome.

Nun hast du mir den ersten Schmerz getan (Now You Have Caused Me my First Pain). This, the final song in the cycle *Woman's Love and Life* is one of Schumann's most expressive and moving pages. The singer treats it all in recitative style, taking her own time, making her own pauses. Her progress, prostrated as she is by grief, is laboured.

Après un rêve (Fauré); *Extase* and *Elégie* (both by Duparc); *Träume* (from Wagner's *Wesendonck Lieder*), all of these cry out for freedom from the thraldom of strict and sour severity.

To play these (and many more examples which I chose from time to time) in two ways—first with rigorous uniformity and then with life-enhancing *rubato* made the subject less dull, I hope, than the printed page makes it.

David Cairns asserted in a recent article in the *Sunday Times*, on a re-issue of Wilhelm Furtwängler records, that the maestro searched for the composer's deeper will, below and beyond the imperfect symbols that are the notes. He goes on 'If you have been brought up to believe that the tempo shouldn't be changed unless the score says so, it is difficult at first to accept what he (Furtwängler) sometimes does. There was a time when I would have rejected out of hand, without properly listening to it, the acceleration that he makes in the final pages of Beethoven's Seventh Symphony. Now I feel who am I to say that this whirlwind of sound is 'wrong', that it is not obedient to *deeper laws than those of the printed page?*' (My italics).

To return to my lecture. My final 'act' was to introduce a little levity again.

The accompanist, I asserted, should believe in, be living in, the song as much as his partner. The singer has to present the song and his physiognomy must reflect the mood that the words and music are unfolding. If by chance the eyes of a listener stray in the accompanist's direction, the player must look as if he 'belongs'. Not to say, I hastened to explain, that if Loewe's *Edward* was being performed (a frightfully gory ballad of a patricide which abounds with wails of woe and curses) the player should advertise his 'sympathy' by glowering like a werewolf. On the other hand he is not much of a help if he wears an inane simper. This led me to one experience I had when witnessing (I used the verb advisedly) Schubert's *Erlkönig*: the accompanist was more interested in convincing the audience that he could play this difficult piano part without a care, than with the mood of terror he was supposed to convey; his smile was redolent of pleasurable ease as his octaves portraying the galloping horse's hooves rattled away merrily.

The counterpart to this example was to caricature the accompanist with grim visage (in fact looking as he ought to have looked for *Erlkönig*) playing the Richard Strauss *Ständchen* (Serenade). The impression of playing with pleasurable ease would be acceptable here, not, be it understood to show off the player's cleverness, but simply because the mood of the song is so joyous. In fact the player is concentrating as is his habit, but he gives the impression of relaxed serenity, for the deliciously bubbling accompaniment does attract attention and if the player looks taut, his anxiety will be communicated to the listener, who will sit apprehensively on the edge of his seat with the thought 'This fellow is not going to make it'.

* * *

Although I kept several lectures on the go, it was the outline described above that was most in demand. I was able to vary it by giving many different illustrations on the piano and by introducing a variety of subjects: transposition, balance, adaptability (give and take), unwonted experiences (or should I say unwanted); and sometimes interesting questions were put to me.

For the accompanist to stand up and look the audience in the face is a radical reversal of his usual procedure. Singer, violinist, violon-cellist, oboe or clarinet player face the public as they are working. They can be disturbed. The pianist never looks at his public as he plays.

Victoria de los Angeles, as I shall tell, liked a darkened auditorium to aid her concentration. I caught Peter Dawson, on one occasion, after his first group of songs, peeping with umbrage through a hole in the curtain, because he spotted a man in the third row looking utterly bored; never applauding. 'I sang right at him with no effect whatever.' After the next group I asked Peter how he was getting on with his die-hard in the third row—'He walked out' was the reply. When lecturing I have seen a walkout but did not let it disturb me; after all not every-body loves me, perhaps too, the poor lady had to forfeit my pearls to catch a train.

I cannot remember feeling any trepidation before embarking on two hours—including interval—of my entertainment except when I was talking to children. One can get away with murder in front of an adult audience: I have heard 'phoney' performances, seen obvious 'putting on of airs' which have been swallowed hook, line and sinker by the general public. Children can see through these pretensions in a moment; their eager and generous enthusiasm is instantly deflated by the slightest hint of affectation.

Perhaps my lack of nervousness was due to confidence in the value of the message I had to deliver, a confidence which grew when I could feel positive friendliness welling up from the audience. It was a *rapport* far more intimate and palpable than I had ever experienced at a formal concert and it enabled me to change mood from gay to grave without difficulty.

Possibly I started my lecturing with the idea of waging a campaign on behalf of the accompanist but it did not develop that way when I got into the swing of it. After all I am not a disgruntled accompanist and I found myself speaking only of the enjoyment of music and how the listener would find additional pleasure and deeper interest from some of these marvellous piano parts, if only he did not shut his ears to them.

The title of Lecture Recital is perhaps too pretentious for these illustrated talks, yet in spite of my free and easy approach I was very particular over the 'stagery'. Every performer knows how essential it is to be separated from his listeners when he is working and we all find ourselves dreading to sing or play in a salon where our audience is within arm's length. It is the same with lecturing; the speaker must be on a stage and well-lighted. For my part, much of my work was done sitting at the keyboard and it was essential that my audience should see my face, not only because of my histrionics (!) but because if you can *see* your speaker you will hear him the better.

A good piano on a well-lighted stage was all I asked, and it was fatal if, by any chance, my agents had neglected these conditions. At one music club I was greeted by the secretary with 'Mr. Moore, with great difficulty I found six or seven strong young men to lift the piano from the stage to the same level as the audience, it will be much more informal that way'. 'It will kill me,' I answered. 'When I am sitting at the piano only those people in the front row will see me. Please ask those six or seven strong young men to lift the piano back on to the stage.' These stalwarts did it and I was grateful for all their unnecessary exertion. I was not popular with the secretary but shed no tears over that.

Fire and Water

VICTORIA DE LOS ANGELES, as I have said, preferred to sing in a darkened auditorium and the man who saw to it that her wishes were carried out was none other than her husband, Enrique Magriña. He was her 'lights manager'.

The two elements in the title are truly inseparable from the episodes that follow. I might even have called this little diversion 'Firewater', the strong liquor for which Red Indians craved in the days of the Wild West, but that would suggest that Enrique was an intemperate individual. This he most certainly is not. Good wine he enjoys in moderation; his one excess I should say is cigarette smoking and I hear in his company the click of his lighter at regular intervals.

Elsewhere I intimated that he employs a secretary to help him in the management of Victoria's affairs whose duty, I am convinced, is to destroy all letters unopened. How Victoria's world tours are ever envisaged and finally clinched is a mystery. When I introduced them to Fritz Ganss, E.M.I. representative in Germany, who wanted to make recording arrangements with Victoria and Fischer-Dieskau for duets, I said to him in front of Enrique and Victoria 'Make your bookings now while these two are in Berlin for Enrique will never reply to letters or telegrams.' Victoria laughed incredulously—she did not believe me.

I once asked David Bicknell, Manager of International Artists Dept. E.M.I. and a great personal friend of the Magriñas, if he ever had difficulty in regard to correspondence and making recording arrangements with Enrique in Barcelona. David replied, 'In all my life I do not remember ever receiving a letter—even in answer to a pressing question—from Enrique. But I am still fond of them both.' So far as I am concerned, to resort to modern jargon, you can say that again. In fact Enrique is the embodiment of an Englishman's definition of *mañana*. I would almost say he invented it.

He is a most likeable man. This is a trick he played on me. We had just finished a de los Angeles recital on television under the direction of Patricia Foy, and Enrique held a pile of music in his hands and asked me if I would mind holding it for a moment. He placed it on my two outstretched hands and immediately took it all away except for the bottom piece of music. But it was not a piece of music, it was a beautiful Spanish silver tray on which was engraved in Victoria's handwriting 'Dear Gerald, you were *never* too loud. All my love, Victoria de los Angeles.' That exquisite signature of hers with its scrolls and curvilinear flourishes! Could any gesture be more delightful or be more gracefully effected?

On all our tours, Victoria and I spent very little time rehearsing (I did not mind this provided I had had the opportunity to study her programme thoroughly on my own) but more remarkable was her aversion to rehearse in or even see the hall she was going to appear in, even when the theatre was strange to her. At Rosehill where we stayed as guests of Nicholas Sekers, the concert hall was in the grounds and I shall never forget Miki's amazement that Victoria would not walk across the lawn to have some idea of its acoustics and intimacy. It follows that wherever we went, it was incumbent on Enrique to have a 'lights rehearsal' with the manager or electrician: for Victoria does not mind how brilliant the light on the stage is, but she objects to too much illumination in the auditorium, maintaining that if she can see the faces of her audience too clearly it disturbs her concentration. In Florence, Enrique, knowing I was going to the hall in the morning to practise and familiarize myself with the piano, asked me if I would give instructions as to the sort of lighting Victoria wanted. Now I knew this involved a long argument and took time and interrupted work which was vital to me and was more important, I felt, than his repose or the study of his stamp collection. No doubt these matutinal theatre visits were irksome to him but I told him he must be present himself. So he came and at long last had the lights in the body of the hall lowered to his liking. The sponsor of the recital, however, objected that the words in the programme would be unreadable in such dimness. 'I will see for myself,' said Enrique and taking a programme in his hand he more or less disappeared into obscurity. By this time I was getting interested and stopped practising. There was a long wait and a silence, and presently in the distant gloom a little glimmer of flame appeared: it was Enrique's cigarette lighter and he called back to us 'I can see to read the words quite clearly.'

So much for the fire—now for the water.

At all recitals, Enrique is waiting in the wings with a glass of water for Victoria to sip between groups—and at Covent Garden, La Scala, Teatro Colon, the Met—there he waits—ready and willing.

It was at the Metropolitan, New York, that Enrique really distinguished himself. Whether the opera was *La Bohème* or *Butterfly* it hardly matters now, but Enrique had seen Victoria off—or rather on— at the Prompt side, he knew that fifteen minutes later she would make her exit on the OP side, and thither accordingly he wended his way, carefully holding the precious glass of water. He knows back stage at the Met as well as any loving husband, but even so you have to tread lightly and watch very carefully where you are placing your feet on account of the spaghetti-like tangles of electric cables for stage lighting. What with the concentration on slow motion, on making no sound, on balance and avoidance, progress was made in low gear. Enrique had accomplished half his expedition when he heard a mighty 'Whoosh' sound: without moving his feet (those damned cables and the trembling tumbler of water) he turned his head and there was the entire audience —diamond horseshoe and all—and every eye was on Mrs. Magriña's little boy. He was discovered! The cast almost stopped singing at the wonder of it all—and Victoria's lovely eyes nearly popped out of her head. But in the meantime the storm centre of it—stood there moveless—frozen stiff. In his own words 'What do I do? Do I go backwards or forwards? I say "Courage" to myself and I glide—bent almost double in an effort to make myself invisible, onwards, forwards.'

That was really the end of the affair or almost, for there is a tiny cadenza. Within two minutes Sir Rudolf Bing, the general manager, came back stage in a fury and demanded of Enrique, 'Who was that damned stage hand walking across the stage with a glass of water?' I take off my hat to Enrique, for his reply was masterly: holding the glass behind him (now empty incidentally, but still clasped in a hot hand) he said after a fractional hesitation, 'I don't know.'

On this high note, the only operatic appearance Enrique ever made, was brought to a sudden and unapplauded close.

Master Classes, 1962–1975:
Swedish Drill

SOME YEARS ago Yehudi Menuhin, knowing I had retired from concert work, suggested I might be tempted to become head of the splendid
Menuhin School for outstandingly promising young musicians, in
succession to the late Marcel Gazelle. It was impossible for me to consider it as I could see ahead of me extremely long periods in Berlin and
Munich under my recording contracts with E.M.I. and Deutsche
Grammophon Companies. His proposal also mentioned parenthetically
that the appointment involved administrative obligations: at this I had
a slight attack of the vapours and croaked for the smelling salts. So far
as I am concerned you can write the verbs 'to organize' or 'to
administer' on separate scraps of paper—cut them into small pieces
put them into a dry pudding basin and after thoroughly stirring turn
out the mixture. However you look at it the result will be 'to co-
ordinate', 'to govern', 'to manage', 'to direct', 'to prepare for activity'.
These verbs make me tremble in my shoes. Henry Fielding surely had
me in mind when he says in *Tom Jones* 'You may call me a coward if
you will, but if that little man there on the stage is not frightened, I
never saw any man frightened in my life'. Naturally I did not go into
such detail with Yehudi, he was paying me a compliment by con-
sidering me worthy and I did not want to disillusion him.

An invitation came out of the blue in 1962 from Mme Madeleine
Uggla in Stockholm to go there and give a master class lasting two
weeks for Singers and Accompanists. At once a slight palpitation
developed (as at the Yehudi Menuhin invitation just mentioned) until
I came to the saving words 'all arrangements will be made before your
arrival; the sifting of applicants, arranging the pairs, the timing, etc.,
etc., etc.'

All my life people have assured me when I was on the brink of a big decision, 'It will be a good experience for you, my boy,' and here in this proposed course in Stockholm was the experience I wanted, the chance to control both singer and accompanist, so I accepted Madeleine Uggla's invitation. It was my Swedish Drill.

The playing of the pianoforte part of a song, of a violin or 'cello sonata can be taught; a youngster can be shown how his instrument in Schubert's *Im Abendrot* (In Evening Glow) or Schumann's *Mondnacht* (Moonlit Night) can evoke a mood that the words inspire, but to teach how to *accompany*, how to achieve a good ensemble, is not possible without the presence of a singer or violinist at the lesson and this is not a viable proposition. In 1949 at the Royal College of Music in Toronto, where I had a class of twenty accompanists, Ettore Mazzoleni, the principal, told me that a young professional soprano would like to sing at the classes. She was a fine singer and well-known, but since she was singing her heart out daily and, moreover, doing it to oblige me, I was reluctant to criticize her before the class. I came to the conclusion then, that the only way to teach the meaning of partnership is for the teacher to have control over both singer and accompanist.

But—and a murrain on it—I must speak first of the trials and pitfalls of running a class without an organizer.

When Mme Lehmann gave public classes at the Wigmore Hall, the sorting out for favoured applicants was done in advance; she even travelled her star pupil Grace Bumbry from the United States, and had a professional, Ivor Newton, to accompany them. Organization was not complicated. It was a class for singers, *pur sang*.

In a class for singers *and* accompanists arrangements are not so straightforward, for each singer has to be provided with a partner, (sometimes they enter as a pair which eases the situation) but generally they have to be paired by the organizer and may well be strangers to one another, and perhaps after they have rehearsed together find they are at odds on musical or personal grounds.

Without a manager in charge the teacher can be embarrassed if he can be too easily approached. At the Dartington Summer School, for instance, where I had the expert help of John Amis in the sorting out process, I was in residence, and young people who had failed the test would come to me with pitiful cries 'I have come all the way from Japan' (Germany, America) 'specially to be in your class'. Not being heartless I would try to squeeze them in. It was wrong of me because being sub-standard they were an impediment, tedious to the listening class and frustrating to the teacher, taking up time that should have been spent on the promising cases. This was proved again at Salzburg where the class in the Mozarteum broke all records in attendance figures and in consequence became decidedly unwieldy.

The martyr, who never gets a square deal, comes to the too accessible teacher with: 'Professor, I cannot sing with this pianist (or play with this singer), will you make other arrangements for me?'

'But, my dear young lady, almost every member of the class is a stranger to me. Now you have just told me you heard me playing for Mme. So and So?'

'Yes, it was a wonderful concert.'

I went on, 'This artist and I were completely out of sympathy. Our dislike was mutual but we are both good professionals and contrived to make music together.'

Another useful gambit in this type of difficulty, was to tell an experience of my early recording days in the 1920s when playing in a small ensemble of strings and woodwind for a famous tenor. He and the conductor almost came to blows; at least they insulted one another to the secret amusement, I am afraid, of the rest of us. 'I have told you twenty times,' shouted the singer, after several waxes had been spoiled 'that I sing this number in strict tempo. Do you understand what I mean by strict tempo?' The conductor, unperturbed and standing within arm's length of the singer called to us, 'Gentlemen, Mr. So and So says he sings this in strict time, watch me carefully for all fluctuations of tempo.' At the end of the session singer and conductor turned their backs on one another. The record was a best seller!

But with an experienced, diplomatic and firm *chargé d'affaires* then 'up my heart and ope mine eye'. All I had to think about in Stockholm was the music—all difficulties were shouldered by Madeleine Uggla.

In fact everything was managed so smoothly that I made no attempt from 1962 till 1972 to find out how the machinery worked. Everything that turns over under the bonnet of a car is a mystery to me and I am not the least bit curious about it; so it is with administration. I am ashamed of this—not about the running of a car but about the classes; accordingly I wrote to Madeleine and she gave me the following explanation.

We tested about forty to fifty singers and thirty pianists who signified their intentions to take part. To select the chosen few we invited a jury of qualified musicians, with the object of accepting twelve couples as participants and two extra couples as reserves. Our applications were from Sweden, Finland, Denmark, Holland,

and U.S.A. This was six months before the first class was to be held.

Five weeks before the course started Ulla Lovberg and I tried to divide the students into twelve couples (one singer and one accompanist) to practise together, trying as far as possible to ascertain they were on speaking terms!

It was my task to help choose their programmes for I wanted them to be varied and interesting from the singer's point of view as well as the accompanist's and the audience's. It would not do to have the same songs in the programme of more than one couple. Imagine rehearsing *Frauen-Liebe und Leben* (Woman's Love and Life) several times during one session!

We arranged to have extra copies of every song that was performed so that non singers and players could follow the score and understand what you had to say, in detail.

Eventually fourteen singers and fourteen accompanists were passed by Madeleine Uggla and her jury in the preliminary tests.

The classes were held twice daily for two weeks—Saturday and Sunday excepted—the morning, in private, in Madeleine's own capacious music room and the evening at a hall near the city centre to which the public were admitted. (We had a page turner, an Australian, Alan Blair, an expert linguist who was able to translate anything I said. He was an institution in himself and a loyal friend.)

Above I used the word 'passed', but with a blush, for some of these were graduates of the Swedish Academy of Music—the oldest musical academy in Europe outside Italy—some indeed were well established singers. Erik Saeden, a baritone of distinction and one of the principals of the Stockholm Royal Opera House was in constant attendance over the years: he had such a fine voice and was so versatile that the opera house was inclined to overwork him (at least in my opinion). Margot Rödin was another shining light of the same company. The modesty these and other fine artists showed in spending their limited spare time during their busy season to sing to me and to stand before an audience who regarded them as stars (as indeed they were) and be pulled up short to listen to suggestions was touching. It was a responsibility and as I am a conscientious musician giving all I could give, I felt exhausted after two days during my first course, and told Enid I could not continue. However, these young people—above all Madeleine Uggla—were so inspiring, the audiences so eager and responsive that I speedily revived and got into the practice and rhythm of it. We were soon all working together as a team.

Presiding over a class in privacy is altogether different from a public class. The people who have paid not only want to hear the music, they want to catch the words of wisdom proceeding from the lips of the master; but the master learns that it is sometimes wise to keep his mouth tightly closed. 'A much talking judge is like an ill-tuned cymbal,' declared Lord Birkenhead (he was a young K.C. when he gave a tiresome County Court Judge the benefit of this precept) and I found it wiser to be economical with my remarks without softening my criticism. When I did give voice I did not indulge in 'asides' to my young colleagues, I spoke clearly so that the paying guests should hear what was being said. One accompanist—it was the first 'turn' after a coffee break—ran to my table and whispered ingratiatingly in my ear, 'Please give me the tempo of this introduction; it will save time.' I replied, 'I'll tell you in the class—that's what it's all about.' The audience plays an essential part in the proceedings; it excites the younger performers, sharpens the teacher, even keeps the experienced singers and players on their toes. Applause was acceptable, naturally. After a phrase had been repeated several times and at last performed satisfactorily the audience's appreciation was encouraging.

It was important that singer and accompanist should be the centre of attraction, so I sat to one side to have a clear view of the two of them, but conveniently placed so that I could, when necessary, go to the piano and accompany the singer. This was done, sometimes to help the accompanist, sometimes to illustrate to the singer an idea that could be better expressed by my fingers than by words. I have even been known to sing—and this took some audacity—but observing signs of amusement on the faces of my hearers would assure them that the more they heard the strange sound I produced the more it would grow on them. We—that is, performers, audience and I—laughed when levity was not out of place because these things should not be conducted in a pompous way. It was impressed on the listeners that whatever laughter might be engendered was shared *with* the musicians and not directed *at* them. No time was wasted in cosseting a performer by my being excessively considerate: if something was bad I said so and we tried to get it right.

A teacher should not be inflexible and insist that *his* is the one and only path to follow, for there are many ways of interpreting what one imagines to be the composer's wishes, and all may be acceptable. 'I like your ideas very much, you sing with feeling and musicianship. To me your tempo—although the instruction is *lento*—is a little pedestrian, too static. You are moving on your heels rather than on the ball of your foot. Will you think about it and repeat the song next time you sing to us?' (A repeat performance is of great benefit but it has to be dispensed with if the schedule is choked by a too crowded class.) A criticism I made more than once was 'You go away somewhere during the pianoforte interlude. You must sing mentally through your non-singing bars,' in this instance the song was *Meinem Kinde* (My Child) by Richard Strauss ('You sleep. and softly I bend over your cot and bless you' are the first lines of William Mann's translation), and one of my young sopranos turned on me after one of these sallies 'But I had not gone away, I was right here concentrating fiercely'. She said it with such vehemence that the audience could not refrain from showing amusement. 'Well,' I said, 'you looked fierce, you gave me the impression that if that baby dared to wake up he would get one hell of a spanking.' My young soprano joined in the hearty laughter.

At one of my Stockholm visits a representative of Finnish Tele-vision sat in the audience for several days and asked me to conduct a class in Helsinki a year later. I accepted, if only to give Madeleine Uggla a break. This engagement under television sponsorship was again for a two-week span and I found myself under the charge of three ladies, Anja Marvia of the Finnish Broadcasting Company, Brita Helenius, television producer, and a gifted pianist Meri Louhos as interpreter. We had the cameras on us most of the time. Being tele-vised was not inhibiting, and for three reasons: everything was being put on film, could be edited, and Brita Helenius (the Patricia Foy of Finland) had such a lively musical mind that it was certain the duller moments would be expunged; secondly some of the choicest of my Stockholm class were there; lastly and most important, everything was spontaneous, by which I mean the programmes were fresh. We did not rehearse *together* before the cameras turned. It was a class not a concert.

To rehearse a class before transmission is a blunder. This was the mistake that was made when I held a class for B.B.C. television. My friend Walter Todds and I fixed the programme and I rehearsed the songs with the singers and players *before* going on the air. I corrected, I suggested. It was fatal. When the tapes and cameras rolled the young people were so acute and responsive to what I had already said that there was little new for me to say. To make matters worse one of the cameras or microphones packed up at performance and we had to start again with the result that a blatant error of musicianship which I had corrected led to an embarrassed young man saying, 'I hate to repeat that bloomer I made, I'll try, but knowing what I know now I shall not be very convincing.'

No, everything in affairs of this sort, *must* be *impromptu*.

I hope that my T.V. Class in Finland made good viewing, but like the conjuror who only made 'one night stands' I skedaddled before the finished product was put on the air. (Should I say before I was found out?) In extenuation let it be said that I am still on the most cordial terms with my Finnish sponsors, and as for the class, they presented me, at a large party on the eve of our departure, with a magnificent Orofors glass bowl which is almost too heavy for me to lift.

None the less I am not convinced that Master Classes make good television. I have watched Maestro Pablo Casals (to whom I was devoted) giving a public class in Puerto Rico and gained little from it. The same can be said of the class of Paul Tortelier, though admittedly he has a more impressive profile than either Casals or I.

Of the American classes there is nothing much to add. They were smoothly organized and enjoyable, being arranged during my peripatetic visits there.

In 1965 I was invited to Japan to give individual lessons in song interpretation. The proficiency of some of the singing of *Lieder* dumbfounded me until I remembered that Gerhardt Hüsch made long teaching visits to Japan, also, that a noted Austrian teacher Mme Schopfer, a friend of Mrs. Stein (Marion Thorpe's mother) was domiciled in Tokyo. Classes were held, after a day of teaching, at Tokyo University of Arts and four other Music Colleges in this teeming city. (I would ask how far from my hotel would this or that institution be and would be told 'About one mile and your taxi will take nearly thirty minutes over the journey but it will be less exhausting for you than walking!')

The classes themselves were hard going, for every word I said had to be translated into Japanese for the benefit of an audience of two thousand keen and deadly serious young people. I liked to lighten the atmosphere as much as possible but this depended largely on the personality of the interpreter; if he or she were relaxed it was a great help—if taut and humourless, an impediment. Women were better than men at this.

On my agenda were seven song recitals with Japanese artists— in Tokyo, Yokohama and Osaka. One of these was with the baritone Eishi Kawamura whose reputation has deservedly spread to Europe and the Antipodes. He warmed my heart not only by his authoritative singing and his excellent German but also by presenting me with a bottle of extremely palatable Japanese whisky. (What can the Japanese *not* make? They manufacture American chewing gum, Mackintosh's toffee, English muffins and Scotch whisky.)

Perhaps my London classes in consecutive years at the South Bank Summer Season gave me more of a thrill than any other. The machinery behind the scenes, was kept running in perfect order—*molto legato*—thanks to the tactful and adroit way that Mrs. Sonia Harris managed difficult details. Also it was heart-warming for me to greet a few faithful followers who came to one class after another no matter where the venue, particularly my dear friend Bo Ohlgren, the singer from Stockholm, who had attended so many of my courses over the years.

Always in these assemblages it was inspiring to feel, day after day, a growing rapport between the young people and myself. We each had our failures on occasion, but we each recognized that the other was doing his best.

Looking back on a lifetime of concert work, lectures, the little private teaching I had time for, recording, I would say that nothing has given me more pleasure or has been more rewarding than these master classes.

Seventieth Birthday Record

'RELAXING AFTER a recording session one night in company with the recording manager, Suvi Raj Grubb, Gerald Moore happened to preface a remark with the common enough phrase "When you come to be my age . . ." Grubb looked up in surprise. He had never thought of Gerald Moore as more than a few years older than himself. He could hardly believe his ears when his companion revealed that on July 30, 1969 he would reach his seventieth birthday. At once Grubb took it as a challenge—and he had only a few months left for the task—to devise a tribute, etc., etc.'

This excerpt by Edward Greenfield was written for the notes which accompanied the issue of my birthday record.

Before Suvi could start the ball rolling it was necessary to have the imprimatur of David Bicknell, of E.M.I. David has been a personal friend of mine for many years and he immediately gave his blessing to the project but told Suvi 'I don't believe for a moment that you will succeed in organizing it in such a short time.'

The fact that he did succeed is, above all, evidence of the esteem in which Suvi Grubb is held by all who have worked with him.

He is a remarkable man. What mystified me until I asked him, was how an Indian could gain such a deep knowledge of Western music; for Indian music is unharmonized and never modulates. But the answer he gave me is surprisingly simple: his family are Christians and he was brought up on hymn tunes. 'I was impressed as a child by the harmonization of "Eternal Father, strong to save",' he said. The first record he bought was Weber's *Invitation to the Dance* (arranged by Berlioz) and the first Symphony he ever heard was Beethoven's Ninth, both records with Leopold Stokowski conducting the Philadelphia Orchestra. (Strange coincidence, for my introduction to a first-class orchestra at fifteen years of age in Toronto was with the same orchestra and the same maestro.)

He now became immersed in music, studying harmony and counter-

point and listening to every record he could lay his hands on, but it was
not until my dear friend Solomon gave a pianoforte recital at the
Viceregal Lodge in Delhi during the war that Suvi Grubb had the
opportunity of meeting a famous artist.

It was natural that he should gravitate to Europe with his wise and
delightful wife and settle in London. Learning that the Philharmonia
Choir needed baritone voices, he obtained an audition with Wilhelm
Pitz and sang in impeccable style and steady voice, 'But who may abide
the day of His coming?' He was accepted and came into contact with
Walter Legge. This was the turning-point in Suvi's career, for it so
happened that Walter was looking for an assistant.

In the course of Philharmonia rehearsals Legge asked him to his
house one evening and put the Indian to a test.

'Tell me the opus numbers of Beethoven pianoforte sonatas.' This
was answered immediately and without trouble.

'Hum the opening theme of Beethoven's Opus 69' (Legge did not
add that it was a violoncello sonata). Grubb sang the 'cello theme.

'How many movements to the Waldstein Sonata? (Here was a
catch. The second movement so called—is an introduction to the
Rondo—*Allegretto moderato*.) The correct answer is two. And this is
what Suvi said.

The questioning proceeded at some length and Walter Legge asked
Grubb if it would interest him to be his assistant, and receiving an
enthusiastic answer eventually engaged him.

Grubb never ceases to speak with enthusiasm of his work under
Walter Legge and he pays tribute to Legge's tireless patience and the
endless trouble he will take in the endeavour to get as near as is
humanly possible to perfection. Over the years, increasing responsibility was delegated to Suvi Grubb and he finally became a recording
manager when Walter Legge went to live in Switzerland.

Gradually artists reposed more and more trust in this unassuming
but authoritative musician, so much so that Lotte Klemperer told him,
'You can get round my father in an extraordinary way—you know
when to stop.' And Dr. Klemperer himself would say on the telephone
connecting his rostrum to the control room, 'Is it as I would like it?'

The recording of the duet *Cinque diece* between Susanna and Figaro
led to a little trouble. Three times they recorded it (Klemperer hated
too many repetitions) and after the third attempt Grubb rang through
to Klemperer: the conductor picked up the receiver and put it to his
ear without saying a word and waited. 'Dr. Klemperer' came Suvi's
voice 'the ensemble between strings and voices is very rocky here and

there. I think we should do it again.' Klemperer replaced the receiver without replying—then said, 'Sir Evans' (it was Geraint of that ilk—no less), are you satisfied?' 'Yes,' answered Geraint. 'Reri Grist, are you satisfied?' 'Indeed I am.' 'Gentlemen,' addressing the orchestra, 'are you satisfied?' 'Yes' was the chorus. 'I myself,' said Klemperer, 'I am satisfied, but we will do it all again because Mr. Grubb likes it so much.'

Daniel Barenboim, Giulini, Janet Baker, Fischer-Dieskau, Perlman, Richter, Gilels are happy to put their trust in this quiet man from India when recording with E.M.I.

This then was Suvi Raj Grubb, who took it upon himself to shoulder the task of preparing my birthday record in a quarter of the time such an enterprise usually needs, of sounding my friends as to their willingness to take part and of arranging their various programmes and time of recording with the ten artists.

Alphabetically the galaxy consisted of Victoria de los Angeles, Janet Baker, Daniel Barenboim, Dietrich Fischer-Dieskau, Nicolai Gedda, Leon Goossens, Yehudi Menuhin, Gervase de Peyer, Jacqueline du Pré and Elisabeth Schwarzkopf. Neville Cardus, the renowned writer on music and cricket, would have called it a world eleven—that is if you allow Moore to creep into eleventh place.

The above was not the batting (or recording) order, for as Edward Greenfield writes further with the issue of the record 'The problem lay not so much in getting the agreement of each artist—like Jacqueline du Pré they all jumped at the idea . . . but in collating concert schedules and air-time tables to see how a complex series of recording sessions could be arranged in a matter of a few months. It says something for the place of London in the world of music today that it was possible to waylay all the artists on home ground, so to speak—the E.M.I. recording studio in St. John's Wood.' I would add that it also says something for the power of persuasion of Suvi Raj Grubb.

One contribution not made specifically for the occasion was Elisabeth Schwarzkopf's. She has almost learned to be in two places at once but not quite and when all preparations were made, she was in America and from there was bound for Japan and Australia. Fortunately Grubb was able to get into communication with Walter Legge who reminded him that sometime earlier Elisabeth had recorded the five *Wesendonck Lieder* of Wagner with me. From these he suggested that we have *Träume* (Dreams) for the birthday collection. (Wagner wrote it as an exercise for *Tristan*.)

It needs superlative control with its long melting phrases, phrases which, when sung by a Schwarzkopf, sound completely relaxed—and this is where the art that conceals art comes in, for it is a supreme test for the singer. To take one instance of the different challenges that have to be faced, *Träumend spenden ihren Duft* (the dreaming flowers bestow their scent) sung *mezza voce* is as protracted as the breath will allow and climbs note by note up to *Duft* and the magic is lost if the singer cannot make the apex the softest note of the group. It is a famous passage anticipated by everybody in the opera, but in this ambience the singer is enwrapped in a warm voluminous orchestral accompaniment where a breath can be taken unnoticed. With pianoforte the singer is exposed and only a Schwarzkopf can do it justice. I recognized the Walter Legge fingerprint in this choice, as he thinks, I hope not mistakenly, that I have the touch that the song needs. The piano part must be dematerialized—unpercussive; it is *molto legato* and the repeated chords, unless sustaining pedal is used with extreme sensitivity, will become too sonorous. The player bears in mind the colour of muted strings and his fingers hint the word *Träume—Träume* in the soprano voice of the accompaniment. (Duparc's *Extase* needs a similar touch but Wagner's repeated and ampler chords present a deeper problem.)

Listening to the result, I feel that my postlude was fairly acceptable, better than my introduction which does not satisfy me. But I marvel again and again at the Schwarzkopf virtuosity.

Victoria had one free day during her only visit to London—she could have recorded in May or June but that would have been too late for a record which had to be issued in July, so the only de los Angeles session had to be squeezed between two recording bookings for full orchestra, taking place afternoon and evening. Music stands, eighty seats, conductor's rostrum and microphones with the exact position of each chair and mike noted, had to be stacked on one side of the large studio to make room for Victoria's and my microphones and the pianoforte. When we had finished, the orchestral impedimenta had to be replaced. Suvi Grubb allowed forty-five minutes for two Spanish songs to be put on tape. We started on schedule and there was Enrique Magrñia, Victoria's husband, on duty with the indispensable glass of drinking water, and we finished exactly three-quarters of an hour later. Suvi afterwards called it a quick sandwich!

I was delighted that Victoria wanted to sing two Spanish songs—in fact Grubb chose these to begin Side 1. And what a rousing start it was with *Malagueña*, a Spanish folk song arranged by Joaquin Nin! 'When I left Marbella, I left behind me a maiden whose beauty dimmed the sun—even the horse was weeping' so runs the first verse, but the music is rampant with vitality and florid with colour; it can be imagined how gloriously Victoria's Mediterranean timbre rang when singing this; as for me I laid about me with gusto, very sorry for the horse but greatly relishing the elaborate ornamentation in the pianoforte, like twenty guitars and the rattling of many castanets.

I have written elsewhere on Manuel de Falla's seven Spanish songs to point out that the music in this *genre* often seems to bear no relationship to the words and perhaps this *Malagueña* is a case in point. You are told for instance, in one folk song, of a lover and his mistress hurling crockery at one another to the accompaniment of the most enchanting music; in another, to the lilt of a soothing lullaby you hear a dialogue between a dying girl and her stepmother who is poisoning her.

On December 30, 1968 we had a notable triumph, three artists recorded their items and each of them was allowed one hour. They had to queue for all the world as if they were in a dentist's waiting room—though I trust the outcome (or should I say extraction) was not so painful. And what names! Janet Baker, Yehudi Menuhin and Gervase de Peyer.

We were due to begin at 10 a.m. with Yehudi, and I arrived bright and early at Abbey Road Studios to find the dear man had already been there for half an hour or more practising. The *morceaux* he was to play were Ravel's *Habanera* and Debussy's *La Fille aux Cheveux de lin* which, without doubt Yehudi, who is an expert at Yogi, could have performed on his head. These are undoubtedly charming pieces but it might be asked why the mastery of this man was being squandered on what are, after all, trifles.

When Yehudi was in his early teens he told me that his function as an artist was to play big works, and although he has recorded small pieces he has rarely included them in public recitals. His métier is the concerto, the sonata, unaccompanied Bach or Bartok. The life of the man has developed on a parallel with the career of the artist for he has a range of interests far beyond the routine of the virtuoso violinist, (Fritz Kreisler expressed his boredom at the eternal round of travel—hotel—concert hall—travel—hotel—concert hall *ad infinitum*), and I would say that Menuhin has devoted much of his life to the benefit of humanity. One thinks of the school he founded at Stoke D'Abernon, of his presidency, involving much time and responsibility, of the International Music Council (a branch of the United Nations Education, Scientific and Cultural Organization). He is taking a sabbatical during the year I am writing this, and will be preparing four or five speeches he has been asked to deliver for the benefit of various good causes.

It would unquestionably have been more to Yehudi's taste to have played a sonata with me but this would have taken up one side of a record. Without demur, or rather with his habitual generosity, Yehudi conformed to the plan and prepared these *morceaux* as meticulously as if he were going to record the Bach Chaconne. That is why he was practising when I arrived on the scene.

After he had finished he lingered in the control room, I afterwards learned, to give himself the pleasure of listening to the sheer beauty of Janet Baker's voice. It is a sound that is absolutely individual—not to be mistaken for another's. I am reminded of how E.M.I. asked me to listen to their record of a tenor who accused the Company of issuing an operatic aria crediting another artist as the performer. As I knew the work of both men I listened carefully before deciding whose voice it was: the record was played over and over again to me but I could not in honesty come to a decision. This could never have happened with that unique quality that is Janet Baker's alone.

I was presented by David Bicknell on behalf of E.M.I. with a stereo gramophone. He came with several records to test the new machine and started with Janet Baker singing Mendelssohn's *O Rest in the Lord* from *Elijah*—'I am convinced,' he said, 'that she is the greatest singer in the world.'

Strangely enough my beloved Schubert is not represented on my birthday record (which explains no doubt why he sent me no greetings) and I wondered whether Janet would sing his songs. Her choice fell on Mahler—and why not, for she is recognized as an ideal Mahler interpreter: the two she chose were *Frühlingsmorgen* (Spring Morning) and *Scheiden und Meiden* (Parting).

My heart was touched by Janet's contribution for I knew that on this frosty morning she had a cold and would have been justified in staying at home in the warmth. I took it not only as a compliment but as a gesture of her friendship for me. As a footnote it must be said that no trace of her indisposition is discernible on the finished product.

The percipient reader is saying 'No mention of rehearsals'. He can be assured that thus far there had been nothing slapdash about our preparations: the songs with Elisabeth, Victoria, Janet had all been performed by us many times and Yehudi's pieces did not require solemn scrutiny or heart-searching discussion but Gervase de Peyer's arrival on the scene at noon was a different proposition. We were to play Weber's *Theme and Variations* for clarinet and piano, the longest title on the record, well over nine minutes. I had last played in concert with Gervase about ten years previously when we joined the Spanish 'cellist Gaspard Cassado in the Brahms Trio for clarinet, 'cello and piano. This Weber piece we had decided on was a first performance for me; as for Gervase he knew it intimately, played it superbly, and was the greatest help to me when we rehearsed—in the quick variations the ensemble is tricky. We could not finish it to our satisfaction (is one ever satisfied?) within the allotted hour but Suvi Grubb was able to arrange a short session for us after lunch: the variations where the piano is solo I recorded the next day.

In the New Year I had to go to Scandinavia for (what is called) a Master Class and after that went on to Berlin to record with Dietrich Fischer-Dieskau and was not due back in England until March. Fortunately Dieter and I were recording songs of Richard Strauss and he suggested two of these for this special record, *Hochzeitlich Lied* (Nuptial Song) and *Weisser Jasmin* (White Jasmin), neither of which could be called hackneyed. The first named has a lovely melodic line with an accompaniment of delicate, delicious (and difficult) embroidery echoing the singer's description of the fragrant acacias, fluttering roses, and compares the bride's tresses to copper beech— then rather suddenly, though with pardonable urgency says *Komm, mein Kind, komm wir gehen zur Ruh*. The sentence is not without poetry but when translated into English reads 'Come let us to bed' which seems a trifle abrupt to me. However, the song has three verses so it seems the bride is not consumed with such impatience as her spouse.

Dieter and I recorded in the course of 1969 all the Strauss songs—a thrilling and terrifying assignment which I mentioned in my Recording chapter.

For some time Suvi and I had deliberated as to what sort of *Finale* would be suitable. One suggestion, not mine, was that I should play something on my own, but I felt this would be out of character. Then the idea came—why not a duet with Daniel Barenboim? Jacqueline du Pré the 'cellist was booked to record the *Elégie* by Fauré with me on April 1, could not Danny come along too and quickly polish off a Dvořák Slavonic dance with me? And it was so!

I cannot improve on Edward Greenfield's account of that evening's session:

> Jacqueline du Pré and Daniel Barenboim, husband and wife, both came to the E.M.I. studio . . . to record their contributions . . . Barenboim had already spent six hours that day rehearsing the English Chamber Orchestra immediately before their world tour together, but he showed not a suspicion of tiredness when in the

middle of Jacqueline's recording of the Fauré he burst into the control room.

Behind his contribution there was something of a plot. Normally when playing piano duets with his father (present in the studio on this occasion) Barenboim plays *primo*, but this time in Dvořák's G minor Slavonic Dance he firmly insisted on taking *secondo* below Moore. He wanted, he explained, to make sure that for once Moore had the tune to play. And then after his first run-through there came the pay-off he had been preparing for weeks. Turning round in his seat he was able, with a beam of triumph, amid Moore's delighted confusion, to ask the classic question, 'Am I too Loud?'

More than any words from a critic these performances, expressly recorded, themselves explain what is special about Moore's playing. During one of the play-backs Barenboim chipped in with an enraptured comment 'What beautiful tone!'— a spontaneous tribute from one pianist to another. 'Steinways always do that,' Moore replied in his down-to-earth way, but he knew well enough how genuine the compliment was.

It was a joy for me to play with that remarkable artist Jackie again— she inspires everyone who comes in contact with her. One thing, however, gave us both some astonishment: Danny said he was hearing the Fauré *Elégie* for the first time.

The picture of us shows Jackie pushing her bow through a hole in the music, a hole not caused by tear or wear (although close inspection shows the page edges are a bit frayed) but by scissors: I had cut out two bars to have them photographed for some article I had written about this classic piece for the 'cello.

Nicolai Gedda came the following evening and this recording was another sandwich, for this renowned tenor came between two performances at the Royal Opera House, Covent Garden. He sang two Tchaikovsky songs (in Russian of course, it is one of the half dozen languages he speaks fluently) *Don Juan's Serenade* and *At the Ball*. The serenade may not be genuine Spanish but the bravado of the Don is brilliantly illustrated with bold singing and a swashbuckling accompaniment.

The inspiration for this collection had come to Suvi Grubb in the Geneviève Restaurant and thither we repaired with Nicolai—joined by Gervase de Peyer—when we had finished, to enjoy a little celebration.

Only one artist remained on the agenda, my old friend Leon

Goossens. In his halcyon days he was lauded as no other oboeist has ever been (one ecstatic admirer actually said to me 'He *holds* his oboe as if it were a sceptre' though even Lee could not possibly play his instrument when adopting this regal pose) and his fellow musicians admire the courage he showed in making a splendid come-back after a motoring accident that badly cut his lips.

We were excellent companions in Russia together with Sir Arthur Bliss's party: Lee had never forgotten how I had the opportunity to pull his leg. Apologizing for being late for lunch one day after rehearsing a concerto with the Leningrad Orchestra he said, 'I was waylaid by the woodwind players who wanted photographs of me and some of my old reeds.' I quickly said, 'They will *treasure* the reeds.' Lee joined in the laughter that this sally provoked.

But he had his revenge now—during our recording of the Bach *Siciliano* (from Cantata No. 29). All the responsibility for the long phrasing and *legato* lines resides in the oboe part—most beautifully accomplished by Goossens. The accompaniment is simple in the extreme, nevertheless in a play-back to test the balance I struck a wrong note, accidentally of course. Leon stopped the record, turned to Grubb and murmured in his soft voice, 'Did you say eightieth birthday?' Touché!

My deep gratitude is owed to these champions for contributing their unrivalled art towards this birthday tribute to me and, of course, my affection to Suvi Raj Grubb not only for his conception but for his patience and his ability to cope with a veritable jig-saw puzzle of dates, times and programmes.

* * *

Electrola (the German branch of E.M.I.) thanks to my friend the late Fritz Ganss, recording manager, also issued a record to mark the occasion, it consisted of titles made in Berlin and Munich during the previous three or four years. All the artists were singers, they were Victoria de los Angeles, Christa Ludwig, Anneliese Rothenberger, Elisabeth Schwarzkopf, Walter Berry, Dietrich Fischer-Dieskau, Nicolai Gedda, Hermann Prey: the issue was named *Meister des Liedes*.

Jackie

UNDER THE AUSPICES of The Arts Council of Great Britain, 'A Gift for the 'Cello in memory of Madame Guilhermina Suggia', was founded, a year or so after the Portuguese 'cellist died, its object was to help promising students of the instrument. John Barbirolli, who was a 'cellist before becoming a conductor, Lionel Tertis, Arnold Trowell and other distinguished string players and musicians were enlisted as a panel of adjudicators under the chairmanship of Eric Thompson, to hear these annual auditions.

When Jacqueline du Pré first appeared in 1956, she was eleven years old, scarcely taller than her 'cello; her auditors were electrified after she had been playing for only half a minute. It was not until her third performance for the panel that I heard her for the first time, she was then thirteen, and it was obvious to us all that here was a genius in the making. I heard this amazing child for three successive years and her talent continued to flame. She was a bonfire.

What a responsibility to have such a girl as this under your musical tutelage! Her teacher was William Pleeth and to this day she is grateful for all the guidance he gave her. Here is an excerpt from his letter of recommendation when she was heard at the Suggia Award for the first time:

> She is the most outstanding 'cellistic and musical talent I have met so far, to which she adds incredible maturity of mind. I am of the opinion that she will have a great career and deserves every help to this end.

I quote this letter not only out of compliment to Jackie but to pay tribute to the generosity and unselfishness of Pleeth. A teacher, once in a blue moon, suddenly finds that a young student under his care is unusually gifted and is sometimes loth to part with him or her for fear of losing the glory that will rub off on to the teacher. Years ago I wanted a young 'cellist to go to Casals for lessons and she was as keen as mustard, but it was a fight to induce the London teacher to part with her: 'What can Casals give her that I cannot?' she demanded of me. Similarly I know of a gifted singer whose brilliant voice is eminently suitable for the operatic stage, but when I made the suggestion to the young hopeful that a year's course at an opera school was essential, I was told 'I shall never, never leave my present teacher.' This attitude is not the fault of the student but of the teacher.

One can say that William Pleeth taught Jacqueline du Pré wonderfully and then, when the time was ripe and the moment opportune helped to launch her into less sheltered waters to broaden her outlook and enrich her mind.

By the expression 'less sheltered waters' I am not suggesting that when she went to Moscow to study with Mstislav Rostropovitch he gave her a rough time! He was, as always, an inspiration to the girl and when she returned to England an international career was opening out for her.

She had developed mentally and physically, musically and technically. Beneath the quiet surface were hidden all the emotion, the feeling, the sensitivity of your finished artist. In addition, to give them expression, were a wonderful bowing arm and a string hand strong and sure; intonation impeccable—quality of tone beautiful.

I partnered Guilhermina Suggia (often alluded to as the Teresa Carreño of the violoncello) very frequently and we were great friends, but I think that Jackie's tone had more body. I do not say this to belittle the Portuguese artist, for she would herself have acknowledged it, so ungrudging was she in her appreciation of her fellow players. In fact she played like a woman whereas the English girl had the strength of a man. (To acquire a big tone becomes a fetish with some 'cellists and often—like singers forcing their voices—they gain it only at the expense of quality. Hans Kindler, from the Netherlands, forsook his instrument to become a conductor of the Washington Symphony Orchestra, but in his playing days would pretend to identify rival 'cellists by the size of their tone. 'Do you remember X?' I once asked him: after affecting to cudgel his brains for a moment, 'Oh yes, now I remember him. Small tone.')

Strength, however, was probably the last thing that Jackie thought about when she played, for she was simply obsessed by the music and flung herself into it with utter lack of self-consciousness. I nearly wrote 'with fierce concentration' but the adjective would be false, for I have seen her and Daniel Barenboim at public performance exchange smiles or ecstatic glances during the course of some inspired dialogue between 'cello and piano.

When Daniel Barenboim was first introduced to Jacqueline du Pré at a small private party he said—so I am told—'You do not look like a musician.' The suggestion was immediately made that they play something together there and then to satisfy Danny's scepticism. It is not for me to say that the pianist was swept off his feet for I was not present, but it is a matter of history that the du Pré–Barenboim combination was born at that instant, that it developed into a permanent partnership and that they became man and wife. Further, knowing Danny's absolute identification with Israel, Jackie embraced the Jewish faith. Full and unequivocal commitment. There are no half-measures with this young woman.

There were no half-measures when she was seized by multiple sclerosis; it was not a gradual attack which would enable her to carry on for a few years before it affected those wonderful hands and arms; it struck completely and with devastating speed. And this is where her greatness of soul has won the love of us all, for she has a radiance rising above all physical impediments.

'Wait a moment,' said Barenboim after one of his concerts, 'there is a beautiful girl coming along in a minute', and there she was in her wheel-chair looking at her husband with love and pride, shedding gladness all round her.

And Danny, illustrious musician that he is, wanted everywhere the world over as a pianist and as a conductor, puts his beloved wife first and his dazzling career second. So as not to be too far apart from Jacqueline, he only accepts engagements that necessitate him being away from her for two or three days at the most (Paris, Berlin, Milan) within an hour or so of flying time from their home in London. He and his wife are still perfect partners and no greater tribute can be paid than that. He is worthy of her.

I listened to her melodious speaking voice on the radio recently and her high heart, her love of beauty, were made clear when she told her interlocutor that she hoped to express in poetry what she could no longer express in music. 'But I am very lucky, for the violoncello repertoire is small and I have had the joy of studying and performing nearly everything I wanted.' Sublime courage!

I shall always treasure the moments when I was associated with this wonderful artist; they were all too few, but I am grateful for them.

To Revoke or Renege

AS EVERY bridge player knows, to revoke is to fail to follow suit when you hold a card of that suit in your hand. To do this deliberately would be cheating, but since sharp practice is bound to be discovered by the other players, it stands to reason that when a revoke occurs, it is an accident caused through carelessness, and the offender is penalized. Once in a blue moon the very finest players make this boner—why, even I have made it myself. As soon as you have discovered this card which you did not see you were holding you say at once (having played a false card) 'I am sorry, I have revoked' and your opponents quite happily mark bonus points on their score; your partner also marks them but a trifle sourly since he, like you, will be penalized. In America the verb 'renege' is used instead of 'revoke' and it covers a wide range of interpretation. For instance: 'Did you go to Moore's lecture recital last night?' 'No. I reneged.' This unlike the renege at cards would be intentional, the clever person in other words had ducked out of it.

I thumped my chest manfully when boasting in an earlier chapter that I obeyed the principle 'Stand not on the order of your going, but go at once' but I herewith confess that I reneged—in fact I reneged three times.

Since the appearance in U.S.A. with Fischer-Dieskau in 1967 I had lain fallow, but two years later I had a summer class at Dartington. The evening concerts there are events to remember. During my ten days in residence I heard Alfred Brendel, the Amadeus Quartet, Neville Marriner with the Academy of St. Martin's-in-the-Fields and my dear Janet Baker. Sir William Glock and John Amis, as can be seen, attract the finest artists in the world and the audience is composed of teachers and ardent quasi-professional students. It is a wonderful atmosphere, and I could not possibly resist the invitation to play for Janet.

I have no regrets and—more important—Janet Baker had no regrets either—even *during* the performance.

But this was only the beginning of my defection.

In 1974 I was asked to play in Paris for UNESCO for a concours of the International Music Council. Yehudi Menuhin is the president and it was at his personal and pressing request that I accepted the invitation. It is impossible to refuse Yehudi, always providing it has nothing to do with administration.

We attended a reception almost immediately on arrival in Paris as guests of the Deutsche Grammophon and I hardly had time to recover my breath when I found myself in deep trouble. I was photographed with Régine Crespin, Yehudi Menuhin and Mstislav Rostropovitch, grouped before a huge tapestry which our hostess Elisabeth Koehler assured me depicted a cricket match, and then told me to explain the game of cricket in a few words to these three innocents, who after all had done nothing to offend me. I looked at the tapestry and could not make head or tail of it; the implements that these 'cricketers' were using were unrecognizable and the characters judging by their attire were either preparing for a ball or the Wars of the Roses. Before I had gone half-way through my first stuttering sentence I could see that my trio of listeners thought I was mad. On the proposition that attack is the best form of defence I turned to my hostess and declared that Régine, Yehudi and Mstislav had been inadequately educated. I also declared the innings closed and dismissed the class.

There were two concerts, the first in the Hall of the United Nations. Yehudi played the unaccompanied sonata of Bartok; it is a *tour de force* and takes great concentration and strength to play it. The listener too has to work. Then followed Indian music, singing with self-inflicted accompaniment on *sitar*. *Tabla* and *baya* (drums) were also in evidence. Malcolm Arnold once told me with utter incredulity that Indian music never modulated, so I listened with unaccustomed persistence, willing it to do what it would not. It is beyond belief that the tonic key should hold unadulterated sway for so long, for so very, very long. Knowing Yehudi's interest in it I wondered if it had much connection with Hindu philosophy in which he is absorbed, but if it induces meditative calm I did not get the message; on the contrary I became more and more irritated as it pursued its relentless course. We sat with Wilhelm Kempff and his wife, each of us giving the other moral support, sustained by the assurance that we should hear Rostropovitch after the interval provided we lived long enough.

The entry of Mstislav Rostropovitch was the signal for an acclamation which lasted for several minutes. During the interval television lamp standards had been erected in the aisles and focused disturbingly close to the 'cellist's seat. They were all switched on with blinding power as the artist came in. He seated himself and still smiling pointed with his bow at the lights and shook his head gently to signify he could not play Bach under these conditions. The television men were obdurate, they had never before encountered someone who did *not want* to be televised. Rostropovitch was as firm as they—but he never lost his good humour. At last one light was extinguished to the audience's applause—we were behind the artist to a man. After a minute or so another light was turned off—more applause. In fact the plaudits grew as the lights dimmed. Not until the lighting had returned to normal did Rostropovitch tune his instrument. It was a demonstration of the artist knowing what conditions would be more natural to Bach and getting them without having a tantrum. In actuality it took much longer than it takes in the telling, many prime donne—male or female—would have walked off the platform in a huff. Here we were shown how it could be done without a scene and without giving the audience discomfort. Then Rostropovitch played the Bach D major Suite. His warmth of heart speaks through all his work and it is patent that the inner calm and authority of his playing is carried over into his active life as witness his demeanour in the incident I have described above. Who that heard this performance will forget it? Never can a Bach Suite have evoked such an explosion of enthusiasm.

On the following night at the Salle Pleyel the concert was a miscellany in which my three bewildered friends of the cricketing experience participated, plus Kempff and Fischer-Dieskau. All the playing I had to do was with Dieter in a group of Schubert *Lieder*. The evening was rounded off by a party at the house of Nadia Boulanger.

Although I have had exhilarating experiences in Paris, I cannot say that I set the Seine on fire on this occasion, being a dismal failure as a propagandist for cricket and finding myself in poor form in the songs with Dieter.

★ ★ ★

At Neville Marriner's suggestion I was approached in the autumn of 1975 to produce a group of singers for South Bank Summer Music for the following August, the evening's music to consist of Mendel-ssohn and Schumann songs, duets and quartets. Because of my friend-ship and admiration for Neville Marriner I undertook this assignment on condition that I would not appear as a performer. Fortunately I knew where to start looking, for only a few weeks earlier I had listened to a particularly fine performance by Felicity Lott, soprano, and Richard Jackson, baritone, of Wolf's *Italienisches Liederbuch* with Graham Johnson, piano. The latter is a product of Geoffrey Parsons which is a good enough recommendation. These three artists were forming an ensemble with Ann Murray, mezzo, who was known to me, and Anthony Rolfe-Johnson, tenor. It was these young people who were booked on my recommendation for the concert and I add, without further ado, that they had a notable success. I have no doubt, all being well, that they have splendid prospects in store.

Now comes the final act of my revoking. The last group on our programme was Schumann's *Spanisches Liebeslieder* which requires four voices with accompaniment of four hands on the keyboard. My young friends asked me if I would supply one pair of hands, my own, and join Graham Johnson at the piano. After much hum-ming and hawing I consented but stipulated my name was not to appear in advertising or programme, as a performer. In the pro-gramme notes I played down my part by saying that *primo*'s con-tribution was parenthetical.

Strangely enough, my appearance on the stage of the Queen Elizabeth Hall though unheralded was received with some warmth which was pleasing indeed, though I derived greater pleasure from the feeling that these artists, making their début as an ensemble, wanted me to join them and that they were having a marked success.

This was the last of my reneging.

* * *

Since this event these four singers are the nucleus of a group formed by Graham Johnson named The Songmakers' Almanac and their every appearance is greeted by packed halls.

That I should, in a very small way, be associated with these fine young musicians is most pleasing to me.

Wond'rous Kind

OUR FIRST meeting with Mstislav Rostropovitch occurred a few years earlier than the Paris concert described in the previous chapter, it was at the King's Lynn Festival.

We usually gave ourselves the pleasure, after my little stint at Lynn, of staying over for a few days and were particularly excited to have the chance of hearing the Russian 'cellist. He was to play and conduct a section of the London Symphony Orchestra in a classical programme of five violoncello concertos, three by Vivaldi followed by Tartini and Boccherini for good measure. He was driven down from London and at once plunged into a three-hour rehearsal with the orchestra at St. Nicholas Church; an ideal place for concerts of this nature. It was then that Ruth, Lady Fermoy, Chairman of the Festival, asked us to look after this fabulous man (we were fellow guests of hers in the country) because she had a dozen things to do in the town.

After this strenuous rehearsal we drove him to her house where he shut himself up in his room and practised madly and unceasingly until we drove him back to King's Lynn in time for the concert. It was on these drives to and fro that we began to understand and appreciate this great artist whose buoyancy of spirit, vigour and contagious geniality made us feel we had known him for years.

It was a coup for King's Lynn to procure him, for his visits to England at this period were infrequent and brief and it is possible that his great friends Benjamin Britten and Peter Pears had pulled strings on behalf of Ruth Fermoy to whom they were devoted. Small wonder that Lionel Tertis, King of the Viola, very much a member of the Fermoy coterie, was determined to make the journey from London specially for the occasion. But alas for poor Lionel! He caught a severe cold and, in his ninetieth year, was forced to stay in his hotel room.

After the concert we took Lillian (Mrs. Tertis) to meet Rostropovitch who at once asked 'Where is Lionel?' I explained why he could not be there whereupon he asked if he could go and see him. We drove back to their hotel and Lillian took Mstislav upstairs, while we waited in the hotel foyer.

'Now,' I said, on his return, 'you would like a drink.'

His English at that time was somewhat restricted but he answered without hesitation, 'The same as you.'

'Well, I'm going to have a whisky and soda.'

'The same as you.'

'A large one or a small one?' (I did not really know him that well.)

'The same as you.'

'Mine is going to be a large one.'

'The same as you.'

After embracing us in capacious hugs he entered his car to be driven off to London, waving enthusiastically from the open window until he disappeared. Not a hint of fatigue could be seen after the prodigious exertion the day must have entailed.

A warm humanity flows out of him and is inevitably reflected in his incomparable art.

Lionel Tertis remembered this gesture as long as he lived and, on the last occasion we saw him before his death, referred to it with gratitude.

South Bank Summer Music, 1971

BEFORE JOHN DENISON became General Manager of the Royal Festival Hall—an appointment which he held until 1976 for over a decade—he was musical director at the Arts Council. It was as a member of the Music Committee of that Council that I was impressed by his astonishing gift for administration and his ability to cope with the multitude of problems which came his way. The thought of the homework he must have had to do still makes me shudder. John had been a musician; in his younger days he played first horn in the B.B.C. and London Philharmonic Orchestra. Why do I say *had been* a musician? Once a musician always a musician, and because of this every artist during his reign on the South Bank felt he was under the aegis of a fellow professional. He ran the halls smoothly, firmly and with charm.

South Bank Summer Music was the result of typical Denisonian imagination. His plan was to provide a short season of good music in the Queen Elizabeth Hall during August which was complementary and not competitive with the Proms. He regarded it as a friendly 'getting together' of leading young musicians and he invited Daniel Barenboim to look after the first three years 1968 to 70. He had always resolved, he told me, that the artistic direction should be for a three-year span and when he asked André Previn to take on the next stint, André said he would only do it provided he had time to think up a scheme for 1972 to 74, and in consequence I was asked to bridge the gap.

'I still think your 1971 season was unique,' John wrote me, 'being designed around vocal chamber music and song and if you try to claim that you were only "filling in" between times, I shall say that Providence must have taken a hand in making that possible.'

John's choice of Daniel Barenboim to launch the series was brilliant; his fame as a pianist and conductor is international, moreover it would be certain that colleagues far and wide would be keen to enlist under his leadership so greatly do we esteem this prodigious young man—still in his thirties.

Barenboim explained John's idea of the triennial change at a press reception before the start of his last season. I heard myself calling out when he had finished his speech 'Mr. Barenboim I would like to ask a question. Do you feel you are too old to carry on?' I cannot recall if there was an answer.

Although I came in for a certain amount of *réclame* when I took over in 1971 it was Anthony Steel, the planning manager, who shouldered the responsibility. Anthony with whom I was mostly in contact was a steadying influence—always unruffled, always giving the impression that all was going according to plan even when the inevitable contretemps (of which he kept me in ignorance) occurred.

I naturally attended all the preliminary conferences, which included Emmie Tillett, in John Denison's office but once the season started I had no cares so far as administration was concerned; in truth I had quite enough on my hands with my three-hour classes each afternoon, enjoyable though they were. Of course it was my very great pleasure to sit in the Queen Elizabeth Hall every evening for the concerts.

The title of South Bank Summer Music was changed during my régime and was known as South Bank Summer Song 1971. I was called Artistic Collaborator, an appointment which, with but one withering exception seemed to meet with general approval. This one contumelious voice, heard by me alone, telling me I was the weakest link in a chain of distinguished men, necessitates a digression.

I said of myself in *Am I too Loud?* that the elephant never forgets; therefore, taxing the reader's patience I must ask him to take a step back with me into the dim and distant past—a mere matter of half a century—and he will thus understand the delicacy of my susceptibility.

A spinster aunt of mine whose affection or ambition for me seemed to manifest itself in a disparaging manner, had the habit of asking me with monotonous regularity 'When are you going to become a solo pianist?' The shaft—for I knew it was intended as such—would be delivered with a seraphic smile, which expressed even more certainly than words that I was obviously not the stuff of which heroes are made. These innuendos had the opposite effect from what was intended, for I took an unkind pleasure in defying her and by remaining 'only' an accompanist. Even in this capacity, however, my name gradually became fairly well known in musical circles. Nothing daunted, my nonagenarian aunt still retained her stamina, her ever vigilant spirit ready to attack without provocation: 'I see,' she said, 'that so and so is giving a violin recital at the Queens Hall with another pianist. How is it'—settling herself more comfortably with that sweet but derisive smile trembling on her healthy cheek—'that *you* are not playing?'

My dear aunt has now departed from the scene but, as everyone has always impressed on me if I showed signs of complacency, no one is indispensable. Sure enough the old dear has been supplanted by an elderly friend—a lady of course—whom I see on occasion and whose self-imposed task it is to pulverize whatever remaining confidence I have. On hearing I was the intended (to give myself the full treatment) Artistic Collaborator for 1971, she said to me during Danny's season, 'How marvellous the magnetism of Mr. Barenboim! Out of personal admiration for the man and as tribute to the artist, famous musicians from all over the world are flocking round him to participate in his concerts.' Now all this is true and I subscribe to it (in fact I was one of the Barenboim coterie) but there was a sting here which I was meant to take to heart, a sneer behind that most angelic of smiles I was meant to apprehend. The message was 'They will certainly not come flocking around *you*.'

Charles Morris, another nonagenarian, wrote:

> But in London these devils so quick fly about,
> That a new devil still drives an old devil out.

My aunt had a worthy successor.

Yes, I was happy to be one of the Barenboim team. Early in 1969 he had telephoned from New York to urge me to do a two-week master class in August for singers and accompanists, but I had to refuse as I was booked for the Dartington Summer School which was already dealing with candidates. I accepted Danny's invitation for the following year, 1970.

My season in 1971 was designed, at John Denison's suggestion, around vocal chamber music (ensembles) and solo song.

Without going into too much detail I would like to give an outline of the programmes beginning with the sopranos, though this is not the order in which they were presented.

* * *

Oh would I were but that sweet linnet!
That I had my apple tree too,
Could sit all the sunny day in it,
with nothing but singing to do.

                              Air: *The Pretty Girl Milking the Cows*

This verse by William Smyth was set by Beethoven for vocal duet, violin, 'cello and piano. (There is a record of it with Victoria de los Angeles, Dietrich Fischer-Dieskau, Eduard Drolc, violinist, and Irmgard Poppen, violoncellist, and I mention it specially to draw attention to the 'cellist, the late Irmgard Poppen for whom Enid and I had the deepest affection. She was the beautiful, accomplished and devoted wife of Dietrich Fischer-Dieskau and the mother of his three fine sons.)

I am not suggesting the jingle should have been the symbol for my concerts but it is quoted in connection with a friend who happens to be Sweden's reincarnation of Jenny Lind (Jenny Lind is described in Grove's Dictionary of Music and Musicians as 'a soprano of bright, thrilling and remarkable sympathetic quality . . . respected and admired by all who knew her, the mother of a family . . .') no less than Elisabeth Söderstrom. The panegyric on Mme Lind exactly describes her present-day counterpart.

I was playing some years ago at the King's Lynn Festival and Ruth Fermoy asked me to meet Miss Söderstrom at the station; I conducted her to my car and turned to look after her bags when I suddenly heard the strains of 'that sweet linnet' which I had arranged for solo voice and piano, being softly sung by my fair lady. The compliment charmed me for I felt, immodestly, that Elisabeth meant it for me rather than Beethoven. I have been charmed by her ever since and particularly by her recital with Martin Isepp at the South Bank Summer Song, the more so as she made the journey from Stockholm for the occasion.

Another concert was the Sheila Armstrong–Radu Lupu; Gerald English–John Constable recital. Lupu played three Brahms Intermezzi but I was especially interested to hear him accompany the voice. I have followed his career with intense interest ever since I was on the Adjudicating Panel at Fort Worth, Texas, when he won the Van Cliburn Competition. His partnering with Sheila, whom I first admired when she won the Kathleen Ferrier Scholarship some years ago, was impeccable and he obviously relished playing for her.

I have not finished with these sopranos yet for we had Heather Harper in a Bach evening and members of the Academy of St. Martin's-in-the-Fields directed by George Malcolm who also played the harpsichord. As I heard Miss Harper, I experienced a feeling of personal regret that I had not partnered her more frequently. I have listened to her so often; her singing with Peter Pears and Dietrich Fischer-Dieskau in Benjamin Britten's *War Requiem* in Coventry Cathedral is never to be forgotten. But I did have at least one exhilarating 'go' with her when we broadcast William Walton's Cycle *A Song for the Lord Mayor's Table*. She is one of our glorious English singers.

After the high sopranos—the mezzo Teresa Berganza, accompanied by Felix Lavilla, her husband. Her programme consisted of *Arie antiche* and modern Spanish songs. How rich is Spain with Victoria de los Angeles, Teresa Berganza and Montserrat Caballé! I have never been associated with the last; with Victoria of course many times as my readers will know; with Teresa once. She is always accompanied by her husband and only joined me when I had a television series *Great Singers of the World*. And I would add we are still good friends.

Tenors were not neglected, for the series opened with Peter Pears and Julian Bream with accompaniments and solos on lute and guitar. J. B. Steane writes in *The Grand Tradition** 'The Peter Pears voice is one of the most distinctive of all the century's singers, and (like Tauber) the only reason why it can hardly be called inimitable is that it has found so many imitators.'

Robert Tear and Thomas Hemsley, 'Tenor and baritone are we respectively' (as the Victorian duet has it), are also pre-eminent artists of remarkable versatility in opera and concert; they joined Angela Beale and Oriel Sutherland in duets and quartets. This bland statement surely does scant justice to Tear or Hemsley: I am sure if I had asked them they would each have given recitals, but with the generosity of true artists they fell in with the general scheme of programmes and merged their individuality into the ensemble. Robert Tear's scope is unending; by a coincidence, while engaged on writing this chapter I lunched with Sir William Walton who told me that nobody had ever approached Tear in his performance of the speaking part in *Façade*—an awesome statement, for the work was composed in 1926 and countless singers and actors have 'tried their hand' at it.

Thomas Hemsley is one of our leading baritones, a fine and sensitive artist with whom I have recorded, broadcast and concertized for many years. Martin Isepp and Brian Lamport were the accompanists.

Margaret Price, another past winner of the Kathleen Ferrier Scholarship, was advertised to sing in this ensemble but she had to drop out

* Duckworth, 1974.

and Miss Beale took her place at short notice. (This was when Anthony Steel's *sang froid* was evident, and reminded me of the occasion when the wife of the star tenor burst into Sir Thomas Beecham's dressing room five minutes before curtain at Covent Garden screaming, 'Sir Thomas, my husband has no voice—he cannot sing—no voice.' 'I am perfectly aware of that, dear lady,' drawled the conductor. 'But has he found it out for himself?')

The recital I anticipated with eagerness was the *Liederabend* with Benjamin Luxon and David Willison in a programme of Schubert, Wolf and Schumann. Only once did I play for Luxon in my last period of concert activity; in the meantime I had heard him in opera, singing and acting superbly, but this was my first opportunity of hearing him in recital. His singing of Schubert's three Harpist's songs and the evocative *Ganymed* was masterly. The *Harfner* (Harper) songs are a test for any artist and I was moved by his singing of them as I was by the feeling in Schumann's *Dichterliebe* (A Poet's Love). The humour of Wolf's *Zur Warnung* (Word of Warning) and *Storchenbotschaft* (Stork Message) was thrown away delightfully. He was partnered to perfection by David Willison, and Luxon recognized this.

The last recital of all was by Dietrich Fischer-Dieskau with Aribert Reimann as pianist. I do not believe he would have sung at this Summer Song Festival for any one but me: he made only one stipulation, namely that he must sing the programme of his choice. I said to Anthony Steel, 'He may sing the First Leader of *The Times* or the Court Circular so long as he sings.' I cannot deny I quaked just a little bit when I read a draft of his programme: the composers were Schoenberg, Berg, Webern and Förtner. But not to worry. He had as usual, a triumph. Everybody went mad—though whether it was over the singing or the songs I cannot tell. I am bound to add that this magician of an artist brought light to bear on these composers that even a stick in the mud such as I, found enlightening and enjoyable.

There are three concerts to be accounted for. A charming collection of Italian and English love songs by the Purcell Consort of Voices under Grayston Burgess: then The Scholars in a miscellany of sacred music of Byrd, sixteenth-century partsongs: a first performance of *Herrick Songs* by Christopher Brown; negro spirituals and jazz.

The third evening I hardly like to mention—it was called 'An Evening with Gerald Moore' and in parenthesis under my name came the bait 'Admission to include a glass of wine.' I was surprised there were so many thirsty people.

André Previn's innings was followed by Neville Marriner, the present incumbent, who has one more year to go at the time of writing. For Neville's successor arrangements are well in hand, with Itzhak Perlman to take South Bank Summer Music into the Eighties.

Competitions

ALTHOUGH OUR celebrated music schools in London and the provinces have long established foundation scholarships to stimulate their students it was only after the Second World War, I believe, that the competition with the dazzling reward and the 'laurel wreath' came into being in England. The famous ones with which I have been associated in this country are the Kathleen Ferrier Scholarship, the Leeds International Pianoforte Competition and, the very latest of all, the Benson and Hedges Gold Award for concert singers at Aldeburgh.

For many years there have been pianoforte, violin and singing competitions in Europe, the Chopin Competition in Warsaw, the Tchaikovsky in Moscow, the International Competition in Vienna and Geneva; more recently the Liszt–Bartok in Budapest and the Artur Rubinstein in Tel Aviv and there are many more. These have all been prominent by the prizes they offer—either big money prizes or the equivalent in lucrative engagements for the winners and runners-up.

Some of my contemporaries are apt to condemn the modern trend for so many competitions. 'They did not have them in my young day, *we* had no big money prizes, we simply had to work and work and wait to gain recognition.' Precisely. The key to the situation is having to wait: surely if a prize and its concomitant perquisites (engagements, renown) enable a deserving young professional musician to get a lift-up on his road to a career it is all to the good. The time element is all important. Undoubtedly the winners of these events would have 'arrived' eventually but only after a considerable period of waiting in the wings. If Kathleen Ferrier had not decided—on the spur of the moment (and almost for devilment, so high-spirited was Kathleen) to compete at the Carlisle Festival for the Silver Rose Bowl we might never have heard of her as a singer. The winning of it was the turning-point of her life; this was in 1937. In 1953 she was world famous—and died. Thank God, she did not have to wait in the wings or we should never have heard of her.

In my early days I did not distinguish myself at pianoforte examinations. True, I was awarded one or two certificates, but you could say I was generally at my worst at these affairs and my worst was pretty dismal. I had the habit of playing with my mouth open looking idiotic and one day I received a salutary lesson in this respect. Herbert Fryer, a professor of the Royal College of Music, was the examiner—my age group would be eight or nine—and without my noticing it he left his table on which his tea was served, came up behind me as I played and popped a strawberry between my lips. The lesson I learned here is—if you breathe properly and keep your mouth shut you will not enjoy so many strawberries.

Having suffered the torment of these exams as a child I have every sympathy for the poor little wretches when I sit alone in judgement on them.

To be translated from an innocent open-mouthed trembling child who hooted treble in the church choir and drank milk, to a tight-lipped judge who had experienced practically everything except folk-dancing took an interval of nearly forty years. Thanks to my magic pen the reader can see I have helped him bridge this gap of four decades without loss of breath and time, in one single short paragraph. The judge is not hard pressed when it is a question of awarding a certificate, he knows in a moment whether the candidate is worth eighty marks out of a hundred (honours) or sixty (a pass). I say 'in a moment' and I mean this: if he is pressed for time owing to a crowded schedule of students, the players he may reluctantly have to cut short will be the certainties—the good ones; under no circumstances will he cut short the uncertain ones and those he positively knows will be failures: they will get their full measure of time to give them every chance to make up lost ground.

When a prize is attached in the way of a scholarship or money the responsibility mounts. At the *Feis Ceoil* (the competition in Dublin) there were two little girls in a piano class who stood out above the others. The question was which should have first and which second prize, so I asked them to play again. One of them had her hair in long ringlets and she it was who suffered a slight lapse of memory in the replay and I awarded first prize to the other. After I had announced the result I threaded my way through the public towards the exit and a lady, evidently the mother of curly-locks, accosted me in offensive terms for having given her little girl only second prize because of a 'toiny toiny slip'.

Each competition has a different purpose. The Kathleen Ferrier

Memorial Scholarship awards a money prize substantial enough for the winner to take at least one year of finishing study abroad and the trustees take the keenest interest (without attaching strings) in the winner's progress until she or he is successfully launched.

If I take the Ferrier Award first it is because it is especially dear to my heart since I was a close personal friend of Kathleen and a colleague. I was in it from the beginning though it was Hamish Hamilton who had the inspiration, energy and devotion to Kathleen to inaugurate it. His chief moral support came from Winifred (Kathleen's sister) and Roy Henderson who had given the singer lessons when she first came to London from Lancashire. Actually the first singer to win a Ferrier Prize was Janet Baker but it was under the auspices of the *Daily Mail*. Hamish Hamilton's idea was a Scholarship and it was initiated shortly after and has been going strong ever since.

Without question the repute attached to the winning of such a competition is considerable and has proved to be a decided stepping-stone for a professional singer. Nearly all the winners for over twenty-two years (it is an annual event) have justified the faith of the jury and some of them are internationally famous. I approached just two of these, Elizabeth Harwood and Sheila Armstrong, and both told me that their reputations were founded when they took first prizes. One does not doubt that with their gifts they would have established themselves eventually but without this award it would have taken them much more time. Surely the same can be said of Victoria de los Angeles and Jennifer Vyvyan, winners at Geneva, of Lupu and Perahia, winners of the Leeds Pianoforte Competition, of Ashkenazy, Ogden and Lill, winners in Moscow of the Tchaikovsky prize.

Candidates' names are unknown to the judges and are identified only by numbers. In the Francisco Viñas Competition at Barcelona which I have attended several times, the jury hear the preliminary round; we sit at the back of the hall with a screen round us, singers being unseen so that there is no possible chance of pulchritude charming our eyes at the expense of our ears. Sophia Loren, for argument's sake, would be passed automatically into the second round if there were no screens. This screening (I repeat for the first round only) is a peculiarity of the Barcelona Competition and I have never experienced it elsewhere.

Long ago Harold Samuel the great Bach scholar (it was said of him that he could play any keyboard work of the mighty cantor from memory at a moment's notice) told me he could not expect to give a fair adjudication without making notes, particularly when it concerned a long list of entrants, and I have always followed his advice. It is a fact that he was judging a large junior class—about twenty-five in all—and had heard most of them. 'Thank you,' he called when one had finished, and rang the bell for the next child to enter; he went on busily writing, 'Play the Bach Gavotte, please,' he said to the new-comer without looking up. At once there came such a hotch-potch from the pianoforte, such a rough and tumble of sounds, bunches of notes slapped down by the palm of the hand that Samuel almost leapt from his chair. His eyes started from his head as he beheld Dame Myra Hess crouched over the cowering keyboard and convulsed with laughter. They were great friends and the competition was perforce delayed for five minutes.

But notes or no notes, mistakes or misjudgements from time to time are inevitable. The judge and the candidate are both human and if the singer is the more nervous of the two, they at least are both keenly aware that the decision to be made is final—no court of appeal. For instance at the Barcelona Competition a young lady from Dublin won a special prize and when I met her afterwards I advised her to enter for the Kathleen Ferrier Award: 'But I was in it last spring,' she said, 'and did not get through to the second round.' There was nothing for me to say. I do not disclose her name but am happy to relate she is making a successful career in opera and concert.

The Jurors of the Ferrier Award are distinguished musicians—the personnel is changed each year—but for some reason unknown to me I seem to be permanent chairman of the panel. More than once after expressing my appreciation to the Arts Council of Great Britain for the use of the Wigmore Hall I have thanked the audience for the warm reception they accord the jury when we appear on the platform for the presentation of the prize (one of these days we must arrange a recording of the Introduction to *Die Meistersinger* to be relayed as we process down the aisle of the Wigmore), I have voiced my doubts as to whether we shall be so popular when the result is announced. In fact I was so foolhardy recently as to quit the hall by the main door when I was attacked in the foyer by the outcry, 'Every single person in the hall—with the exception of the members of your panel—knew that number ninety-three was the winner, or should have been. She had the loudest and the longest ovation.' Fortunately I had run up against this form of protest at other competitions and had my answer ready, 'Madame, we have no means up there in the gallery of the hall for recording decibels for volume of applause or a stop watch to time the duration of it.' Moral: leave the hall by the stage door.

The Leeds International Pianoforte Competition was instigated by two courageous musicians, Marion Thorpe whose father Erwin Stein was a noted musicologist in Vienna, and Fanny Waterman who has won a reputation as one of our finest pianoforte pedagogues in England.

This competition is known throughout the world and is on the same plane as the Tchaikovsky in Moscow and the Chopin in Warsaw. It was founded in 1963 and is held triennially, the cosmopolitan field it attracts is demonstrated by the scroll of winners: Michael Roll of Great Britain, Rafael Orozco from Spain, Radu Lupu, Rumania, and Murray Perahia, U.S.A., and the last name to be added to this roll of honour was a Russian.

The money prizes in themselves are not the be-all and end-all of the Leeds Competition though they are substantial, of more consequence to the winner (and indeed to a lesser extent to the runners-up) are the opportunities now opened to him (or her) of playing with some of the world's first-class orchestras, and of fulfilling numerous recital engagements here and abroad. Only a professional pianist of considerable talent can think of entering; and he has to be assessed accordingly. Even the preliminary test is a stiff one. The name of the winner shoots round the world overnight.

To sit in judgement on this occasion is a great responsibility and I felt honoured to be invited to join the jury in 1975. For me it was an added pleasure, and not for the first time, to serve under the chairmanship of Edward Boyle. An amateur musician, Lord Boyle has an encyclopaedic knowledge and his deep love of music profoundly impressed the jury: in short he, for all his modesty was an inspiration. It was he who defined clearly that the jury should take into consideration *professional dependability*. This ukase embraces the candidate's performances on each occasion (he will have been heard at least four times) but it goes further in carrying the jury's conviction that the winner, inundated with engagements and new pressures will be able to stand up to them.

The winner of the 1975 Leeds, was the Russian pianist Dmitry Alexeev. There was no discussion so far as he was concerned for the jury voted unanimously for him. Only for the allocation of the remaining five prizes was discussion necessary and I may say it was carried out *senza rancore*.

Going back to 1966 I was invited to sit on the jury for the Van Cliburn International Piano Competition at Fort Worth, Texas. This again is only for the highest standard of pianism. While it does not enjoy quite the prestige of the Leeds and one or two others, it offers the biggest prize money of the lot.

There were several old friends of mine on the panel, Boyd Neel, Dean of Music University of Toronto, Beveridge Webster, a professor of the Juilliard School of Music New York, Friedrich Wührer, respected German pianist, the charming Alicia de Larrocha from Spain, and other notable European musicians. By common consent our chairman was Dr. Howard Hanson from the Eastman School of Music in Rochester, N.Y.

(Although he was not on the jury, the music critic of the *Washington Post*, Paul Hume, listened to all the candidates. Between sessions, Beveridge, Boyd and I played several rubbers of bridge with him. He it was who, after giving a young soprano an unfavourable notice was threatened with a punch on the nose by the girl's father who was none other than Mr. Harry Truman, President of the United States of America.)

The local celebrity, the conductor of the Fort Worth Symphony Orchestra, Ezra Rachlin, was out of courtesy invited to be an ad-judicator and he had more to say, to object to, and propose than any of us. At the first meeting of the panel he seemed to want to usurp the chair and Dr. Hanson a musician of experience, respected by us all, threatened to resign: this we unanimously refused to allow. After this, things went more smoothly, Rachlin was given the task of announcing each contestant's choice of programme for the jury's and public's benefit. His being the only voice to be heard at all the sessions, he was happy, and announced everything well and clearly.

Our respective findings were computerized, the first time I had been introduced to a computer at a competition. The first round proper, if I remember rightly, consisted of some fifty or more pianists. There were four stages (or heats) before the final round, when the jury's sifting would leave six pianists to perform a concerto with orchestra. From these would emerge the winner, and for the judges each succeeding step was more difficult than the last. It will be observed that I stress the task of the jury and say nothing of the sweat and strain endured by the young competitors; this is not necessarily lack of generosity, it is merely that sympathy (or humanity if you like) must on no account be awakened, a player is judged by his performance and nothing else. A pianist from Israel or Vietnam living under fearful tension in his own country, with quiet study and concentrated practice subject to frightening interruption, had to be appraised by the same standard as a player from Los Angeles or London.

Radu Lupu was the winner. I regarded him from the first moment I heard him as an artist with a mind and imagination so exceptional that I found myself more and more impressed each time I heard him. His marks in the computer were emphatically well clear of the others. Now in some competitions I have seen members of the jury 'lobbying', suggesting to their fellows that this or the other should be the winner, but there was nothing of this sort in Fort Worth; certainly I kept my own counsel. When the result was made known to the jury in committee everybody was pleased, so decisive were the figures—everybody but Ezra Rachlin who was the only dissentient and declared that the rest of us were crazy and that the prize should go to another. But I called out, 'It is settled and we are all in agreement.' Actually Rachlin championed a very fine pianist who had incredible dexterity and was a runner-up. As we walked into the hall for the presentation I said to him, 'You are displeased with the result.' 'You're goddam right,' he said. Always glad to be conciliatory I said, 'Well, your man certainly would have won if we are to judge a player merely by his speed.'

My visit to Fort Worth was wholly delightful and was not at all marred by my little brush with Mr. Rachlin, with whom I had been on amicable terms up to the moment when the name of the winner was declared. But I felt a slight diminution of ardour some two years later and it concerns the administration (a word so dear to my heart) of the Van Cliburn Competition.

One of the officials in 1966 was Mrs. G. W. Lankford who organized the jury and became our shepherdess once we were gathered in Fort Worth. She saw to it that we were all present and correct, and generally stage-managed us. I had met her previously in Europe when she attended various competitions. I learned to my regret that Mrs. Lankford had since died, and who should succeed her in office but Ezra Rachlin—the man who likes speed. In the interval between competitions—they are quadriennial—Rachlin held a roving commission and toured Europe as had Mrs. Lankford. What should I read in *The Times* one morning but an interview he gave in which he declared quite outrageously that the jury of the 1966 competition was unbelievably bad. My satisfaction can be appreciated when a year or so later the winner of the Leeds International Piano Competition was announced—and I was *not* on the jury that year. And who was the winner? Radu Lupu. Perhaps my distinguished colleagues at Fort Worth in 1966 were not so crazy after all.

★   ★   ★

Every professional knows when he steps out on to the stage that the first essential for him, before one single note has been played or sung, is Concentration; every other consideration except what he is about to do must be banished from his mind. He has a message to communicate and it is immediate. If he were addressing an audience in a lecture he would find it comparatively easy to grip his listeners at once, provided he had something of interest to say. The musician, the intermediary between composer and public, has indeed something of interest to say for his script is written by a master.

Often the difference between a fine artist and a second rater is that the latter will take much longer to get into his stride—his concentration has not been focused. Concentration is the thing!

There is a parallel in the performer or comedian of the old variety theatre. His act might be timed to last ten or twelve minutes; he could not afford the luxury of allowing himself 'time to settle down' and gradually get into his stride, though it is easier for him nowadays by the aid of the factitious microphone. He had to catch his listener by the scruff of the neck immediately.

It is precisely the same with the serious musician; he must assert his authority at once.

The pretext that many of us make after an unsatisfactory performance is that we were prevented from giving of our best because of nervousness. Our concentration was frustrated by nerves; a shallow excuse coming from a professional and one should be ashamed to take consolation from it. One envies the artists who confidently tell you that they never suffer from this complaint, but one also doubts them. I have come to the conclusion that 'there is no cure for this disease' though I should add the rider that there is this possibility to be considered: supreme concentration keeps nervousness at arm's length.

Why am I sermonizing like this in a chapter entitled 'Competitions'? For the simple reason that it applies to the entrant at a local music school examination or to a brilliant competitor for a big prize. The judge's interest must be aroused at a stroke. Judges are human beings and are as impressionable as anyone, to the immediate impact.

Lionel Tertis, in his nineties, was sitting beside me when we were hearing a young 'cellist of some fourteen summers competing in the Suggia Award and the boy had been playing for less than a minute when the fiery Tertis turned to me and hissed 'This boy is asleep'.

Surprise! Surprise!

THE LUNCH-HOUR concerts at the National Gallery during the war were founded by Dame Myra Hess and there were hardly any first-class musicians in the country who did not welcome the invitation and appear at them. Was there any other British musician with her *réclame* who could have launched this project and given so much time and care to its promotion? She herself must have played—and I am guessing—somewhere about three hundred times and every time was an occasion.

After the war I was guest speaker at the annual St. Cecilia's Day Festival Dinner (in aid of the Musicians' Benevolent Fund which was a beneficiary of these concerts) when Dame Myra Hess was in the chair, and referring to these historic lunch-time recitals I said, 'Everybody speaks of four Landseer Lions at the plinth of Nelson's Column, but they cannot count. There are five lions in Trafalgar Square—Myra is the fifth.'

Not to be mentioned in the same paragraph but the artist who came second in the number of National Gallery appearances was the writer; in fact I scored over a century.

At one of these, Myra sprang a surprise on me—and she was an expert in providing the unexpected, as instance her prank with Harold Samuel I related in the previous chapter. The particular concert took place in the air-raid shelter in the basement—an emergency retreat only adopted when enemy activity was unreasonable, not to be compared in atmosphere or spaciousness with the gallery above. I was associated with the brilliant 'cellist Eileen Croxford when suddenly, at the end of our first sonata and before we could leave the stage Myra strode on and after a charming little speech presented me with a silver Georgian cup on which was inscribed 'To Gerald Moore on his 75th concert at the National Gallery. Our love and gratitude. Myra. July 6th 1943'.

There came a time later in the distinguished pianist's career when she found it a strain to commit some of her repertoire to memory and elected to play from the score. There is nothing to be ashamed of in this if it takes the edge off painful anxiety but it certainly astonished the public when she drew attention to it by telling them, 'It makes it all so cosy.' But it was said with such charm that her admirers loved her for it.

The greatest sensation of all was sprung in Holland and Myra, all unwittingly, was the storm-centre of it. I must relate it as near as I can in Peter Diamand's words, for he was present, or almost present when it happened. Peter Diamand has been presiding over our own Edinburgh Festival for some years but at the time of this particular adventure he was director of the Holland Festival and this is what he told me:

In the course of one of our festivals Myra had given a recital in The Hague. She was staying with the British Ambassador who was a friend of hers. His Excellency gave a party in her honour at which she offered to give an hour's recital before the buffet supper to which I was invited, but being up to my eyes in work at the time, and knowing Myra's playing so well I decided to skip the concert and go to the party when the music was over. I timed my arrival exactly as the guests were moving towards the buffet and joined them. I said to my neighbour, 'A fine recital, wasn't it?' 'Of course, but you with all your experience—have you ever seen anything like this at a piano recital before?'

'Well, you know, I sat right at the back and did not see anything untoward—but then I am very short-sighted.'

'But, Mr. Diamand, you must at least have been startled?'

'No, not at all.'

Very puzzled I approached another aquaintance more tactfully with 'How did you enjoy Myra Hess?'

'Well, I have been to pianoforte recitals for fifty years and never have I seen anything to equal this before—have you?'

'Look at my glasses,' said I, 'the thickness of the lenses. You can see how short-sighted I am and I was at the back of the salon.'

He gave me a searching look so I beat a hasty retreat beginning to feel extremely uncomfortable until I saw an old friend and asked him. 'For heaven's sake, what happened at the concert?'

'My dear Peter you should have witnessed it. One leg of the huge pianoforte went right through the platform making such a mighty bang that we all thought it was a bomb—it frightened everybody out of their wits. Thank God Myra was not injured.'

When recounting this unheard of event I always like to add a postscript to the effect that Peter Diamand there and then, like Matilda's Aunt, decided he must keep a strict regard for truth in the future.

Matter and Manner

PETER DIAMAND'S tenure as director of the Edinburgh Festival began a few years after my innings there of some fifteen consecutive summers.

It was at Edinburgh (and a matter of some self-congratulation) that I once made a remark which amused Sir Thomas Beecham though I did not think it particularly funny at the time. The boot was generally on the other foot, for it was Tommy who, with complete nonchalance, brought gaiety to nations and dismissed dull care.

I had had a morning concert at the Freemasons Hall with a violinist and then repaired with friends for lunch at the Caledonian Hotel. Who should I bump into but T.B., my first meeting with him since his return from a lengthy sojourn in Australia and America. He asked me, seeing I was in a morning suit, where I had been playing, so I had to tell him of my conversation in the cloak room where I was having my coat brushed by the attendant who asked me

'Have you been to a wedding, sir?'
'As a matter of fact I've been to a concert.'
'Was it a good concert, sir?'
'Well, *I* was good.'

To my surprise T.B. was vastly amused and made me repeat the exchange.

Much has been written on the flashes of wit and pungent repartee of Sir Thomas. He made the most of a situation. We read in his *A Mingled Chime** of how he went as a young conductor, with his orchestra, to play at the Cheltenham Ladies College and found on his arrival that the whole school was formed up in the quadrangle to greet him. A comely young lady stepped out of the ranks, embraced him with

* Hutchinson, 1944.
5

surprising vigour and kissed him. Tommy turned to the headmistress, 'What delightful customs you have at this school! Who was that pretty girl?' 'That,' replied the headmistress frigidly, 'was your sister.'

I find this very amusing and have no doubt that T.B. recognized his sister immediately. But the almost sacerdotal atmosphere, the ceremonious army of silent girls was a choice moment for him to drop a little bombshell.

Many of the Beecham sallies are enriched for those of us who knew the sound of his voice and can recall the inimitable expression on his face as he delivered them. There was that moment on television when the subject of the interview was the book he had written on Frederic Delius. 'Was Delius able to subsist on the profits from this orange grove in Florida, Sir Thomas?' 'Dear me, no. He supplemented the allowance from his father, and his tiny income from oranges, by giving lessons to the young ladies of Florida. He taught them composition, he taught them the piano . . . and (a long pause) he taught them *other* things.'

Does the reader find anything particularly funny in this? Possibly not, but hearing Beecham's delivery of 'other things', seeing his eyes rolling heavenwards and the lugubrious expression on his face, I doubled up with laughter.

'I cannot catch what you said, Sir Thomas,' said another interviewer on the radio, 'have you the tooth-ache?' 'Not at all, I am sucking a lollipop.' (One can imagine the B.B.C. man almost fainting with horror.)

The nerve of the man! It was the manner more than the matter.

One item of Beechamania has never, I am sure, appeared in print, it was recounted to me by the late Harold Williams, admirable singer and good friend.

T.B. was in the Antipodes and conducted four performances of Handel's *Messiah* in the principal cities under the auspices of the Australian Broadcasting Commission. All arrangements and advance publicity were in the hands of Roy Lamb, a musical man (he looked after me when I was in Australia) who told me he heard all Beecham's concerts except the final *Messiah* in Brisbane, as he was recalled to A.B.C. headquarters on urgent business. In the course of this performance Beecham—as usual conducting without score—whispered to his baritone soloist:

'What comes next?'

'The Lamb,' replied Harold Williams.

'Impossible.'

'What do you mean?'

'He's gone back to Sydney.'

The only one to appreciate this was the singer who had the greatest difficulty in keeping a straight face.

Music Magazine, 1944–1973

ON SUNDAY the 21 May, 1944, *Music Magazine* came 'on the air' for the first time. Its editors were Julian Herbage who modestly describes himself as having taken 'a fairly comprehensive part in the B.B.C.'s music plans and possessor of a catholic musical taste' (in fact he was a scholar and an authority on English music of the seventeenth and eighteenth centuries, had edited and conducted masques, operas, oratorios by Purcell, Handel, Arne and others and was a composer and author of refined musicianship), and Anna Instone who was a well established producer and broadcaster of gramophone programmes and almost lived among the records of the B.B.C.'s gigantic record library —a professional to her finger-tips.

With unrestrained fervour B.B.C. magazine-type programmes had burst into life from time to time but had all too often lapsed into an insipid rut before the Herbage–Instone partnership came on the scene. Julian and Anna with long practical musical experience behind them, thought deeply for a year before going into action; they laid plans and set out programmes with care and courage. Julian was the right person for the policy side and Anna obviously for the production. They decided that a third person should join the team and they picked a winner in Alec Robertson. Alec was the very man for this informal type of programme, he had a natural way of communication, he did not *address* his radio audience, he chatted with them.

The first point the trinity had to solve was the important matter of a signature tune and here they came to some disagreement. Finally Elgar's Triumphal March from *Caractacus* was chosen for the first broadcast. Whether it was Julian's choice or Anna's, history does not relate, certainly one was for and the other against, with Alec sitting on the fence. In the inquest that followed it was unanimously decided that *Caractacus* was too martial for an informal broadcast, too ebullient for a Sunday morning, when a degree of intimacy was desirable. 'Before many hours had elapsed,' writes Julian, 'Gerald Moore was in a studio at Broadcasting House extemporizing a piano transcription of Schubert's song *An die Musik*. We have since worn out many copies of the record he made on that day.'

(My playing of the Schubert song as a piano piece was indeed an extemporization, but this statement is not a testimony to any particular cleverness on my part. I merely played the vocal line in one hand and the accompaniment in the other without altering a single note of the composer's. Any musician could have done it. It was true I was associated with the heavenly tune, since I used it constantly in my lecture recitals, so much so that in *Face the Music*, the popular television programme, the panel asked to identify it were able to answer without trouble—though Joseph Cooper dryly added in a clear aside, 'I thought it was composed by Gerald Moore.')

Pre-recorded broadcasts as everybody knows can be edited, parts can be expunged, others repeated but, as Philip Hope-Wallace, a frequent contributor to the programme, wrote me:

> We went on the air 'live' after gruelling rehearsals whether the outcome was to be highly professional or flukey 'take a chance' amateurishness. Julian's fervid and nervous punctilio was complemented by Anna's undeviating enthusiasm (at doing a 'pro' job with power). The final run-through once more before going on 'live' was usually as near good as it ever would be. Then the gremlins, shakes, fluffs, ludicrous 'locked in the loo' contretemps started.

Speakers were given as much scope as they pleased so long as music was the subject matter. There would generally be three or four contributors to the magazine who would be allowed a quarter of an hour or so each, and it was always planned that their respective themes were unrelated. For instance if one was an almanac type, celebrating the centenary or anniversary of some celebrated musician (e.g. Scott Goddard's tribute to Sir Adrian Boult on his sixtieth birthday) the following might be a dissertation, again with musical examples played on the piano or excerpts on record of a new work by Britten, Tippett or Lennox Berkeley, and finally we might have Joan Chissell, *The Times* critic, presenting with a critical commentary the latest issue of records (song, opera, pianoforte or chamber music).

If a subject were topical so much the better. For instance the papers had been full of the disgraceful behaviour of the public in Rome when Mme Maria Callas, at a gala performance of Bellini's *Norma* in the presence of the President of Italy, was unable to continue. The great singer had struggled through the first act feeling more and more ill; in the interval with her temperature rising and her hoarseness increasing it was announced that she was physically incapable of going on. All this was in the headlines and hardly a matter for comment in *Music Magazine*. However, three days after the events I have outlined, another soprano was brought in from Naples to take the role of *Norma* for the scheduled second performance and now Julian Herbage took a hand in the proceedings by announcing on the following Sunday that 'We understand Norma service has been resumed in Rome.'

Humour was not frowned on but anything savouring of the high-brow or the patronizing most certainly was. This is illustrated by Martin Cooper, one of the most valued contributors to this pro-gramme. In response to my request he sent me, most generously, the following valedictory note:

> For those who took part in the programme, *Music Mag* came to be felt as a kind of club. One soon got to know most of the Members and the critic's only fear was that he might find himself billed in the same programme as a composer whose latest work he had reviewed unenthusiastically. Anna and Julian Herbage were unfailingly kindly and resourceful hosts—I remember the prompt-ness with which a glass of port was fetched from the duty room to counter a spasm of coughing which overtook me on one occasion. Their tastes were catholic and always open to enlarge-ment; and new music with which neither of them probably had much sympathy was scrupulously represented. The only crime in their calendar I think, was pretentiousness; and I shall never forget the hilarious scenes in the studio—and only just out of sight of the culprit—when one critic insisted against what should have been his better judgement, on playing his own piano examples to illustrate his talk.
>
> The relaxed atmosphere of the programme and the ban on pedantry—the insistence on everything being intelligible to the ordinary listener—was no doubt inherited from the early days of broadcasting, when Alec Robertson and Christopher Stone chatted informally about music and the listener was allowed to hear the soda water squirted into the whisky-glass and the match struck, followed by a moment's silent 'pulling' to make sure that the pipes were alight. That is a style that belongs to the past, no

doubt; and even more recently *Music Magazine* sometimes included programmes that could, with reason, I think, be called dated—reminiscences by early stalwarts of the folk-song revival or contributions by earnest and blameless but also humourless (or worse still facetious) specialists in 'musical education'. However that may be, no new formula has yet been found to replace the old; and I suspect that even now it needs a single personality, or a team like Anna and Julian Herbage to create any comparable institution to take the place of *Music Mag* in the affections of the younger generation of music-lovers.

Yes, after twenty-nine years *Music Magazine* was taken off the air. Three or four months before the last programme I had to make yet another recording of the signature tune since the current record was showing signs of wear. Julian and Anna were naturally with me in the studio and I played several 'takes' so that we could decide on the best. How well I remember Anna's actual words to me, 'I hope the powers that be will not notice how many years we have been running and decide that we have outstayed our welcome.' But her fears alas, were realized and in spite of its continued popularity *Music Magazine* ceased to be.

* * *

A luncheon party was organized by Alan Blyth as an expression of admiration for the wonderful work Mr. and Mrs. Julian Herbage had done. Julian and Anna were wedded during the early days of the run and a blissfully happy marriage it was, though Julian enjoyed calling it 'Quite a marriage of convenience.' The assembly consisted largely of music critics—naturally so for they had formed the back-bone of the programme—and if I had been a young musician I should have been somewhat over-awed, but as I, like *Music Magazine*, had become well advanced in years I weathered it. Besides there were old friends there—Joan Chissell, Alec Robertson, Desmond Shawe-Taylor, Martin Cooper, Philip Hope-Wallace and many others.

Philip was the only speaker and gave an eloquent and witty tribute to the two guests of honour. 'I decided,' he said afterwards, 'to be short and heartfelt—actually I ended up by moving myself.' But he was not the only one to be moved, for we all felt a wrench in saying farewell to what had been an historic feature in the annals of music broadcasts.

In the Chequered Shade

IN HIS book *Music—A Joy for Life** Edward Heath tells us that his Steinway was the first pianoforte to be moved into 10 Downing Street since Arthur Balfour ceased to be Prime Minister in 1906. In my lifetime I have been aware frequently of strains proceeding from this famous address but they were far from being strains of divine harmony. Great leaders have not been noted for their love of music but there are exceptions.

I was engaged to make special recordings in Berlin in 1937 with German singers and I was told they were commissioned by Field Marshal Goering. Again General de Gaulle, after a recital of French *mélodies* sung by Maggie Teyte, talked most knowledgeably about them; he thanked me too for my *sensibilité* though the sceptical reader will say he only has my word for it.

Neither of these gentlemen, however, quite succeeded in occupying Number 10 so I turn to Mr. Neville Chamberlain who was the first Prime Minister I ever talked to. It happened at the German Embassy in 1938 after the Munich 'triumph' of Mr. Chamberlain. The Ambassador Dr. von Dirckson was a charming man and besides paying me a handsome fee for accompanying a German soprano, whose name I am ashamed to have forgotten, asked me to dine with our Prime Minister. After a short recital Mr. Chamberlain advanced to my fair colleague to offer his felicitations but finding she understood not one word of English he had no recourse but to turn to me. He gave me his entire attention and asked intelligent questions about the music; if he had been bored by it then he was a consummate actor.

My second Prime Minister in order of appearance was Mr. Clement Attlee and we met at a Charity Matinee at the Royal Festival Hall. My friend Solomon, the pianist, and I had each performed and afterwards were introduced to Mr. Attlee who was in the act of drinking tea at the buffet. Whether our appearance was frightening or not I cannot say,

* Sidgwick and Jackson Ltd., 1976.

but on hearing our names he dropped his cup and saucer to the ground. 'Dramatic,' said Solomon as he shook the Prime Minister's hand; 'and undrinkable,' I added as I surveyed the glistening tea leaves swimming in the shallow end at our feet.

When Edward Heath became Prime Minister it naturally gave musicians (and I would have thought musicians of any political colour) pleasure to have a First Minister of the Crown who was an amateur pianist, organist and conductor and above all a passionate lover of music. I voiced my enthusiasm to a fellow professional at a St. Cecilia Festival dinner when Mr. Heath was guest of honour. 'Isn't it splendid to have a music lover for Prime Minister?' 'No, it is not,' he snapped, *staccato e marcato*. I told him evidently he put his politics before his music but with me it is the other way round. Surely, I thought, this sourpuss will leave before the speeches but no, he remained, and in spite of a scintillating and witty speech by the principal guest managed painstakingly not to look happy.

Hearing Edward Heath in a political broadcast and hearing him when he is with musicians, one becomes aware that he is two different persons. At the Royal Festival Hall a gala concert was held to celebrate the seventy-fifth birthday of E.M.I. and Mr. Heath spoke at the supper party afterwards. 'That was a superb after-dinner speech—you were in sparkling form,' I told him, and he said, 'I am much happier talking to you people than I am talking to that lot on the other side of the river. But don't say I said that.' So I will not repeat it.

His knowledge of music is really surprising. Edward Boyle gave a party at which I accompanied Elisabeth Schwarzkopf in a recital of Schubert, Schumann, Wolf and Strauss. One of the songs was *Zueignung* (Dedication). Now Elisabeth and Walter had listened to an old record where Richard Strauss, the composer, is playing the accompaniment and he departs—and with good reason—from the written score in the third verse. Here the climax of the song comes on the words '*Heilig, Heilig*' (Holy, Holy) and on this top note, this passionate summit, only one beat is allowed in the composer's original score. Strauss evidently had second thoughts about it for he gives his singer, on this record, a tenure of three long beats and *Heilig* becomes a rhapsodical climax. The Schwarzkopf–Legge combination had justifiably adopted it and this is how we performed it at Lord Boyle's party. Mr. Heath came up to me afterwards and asked me to show him the score and wanted to know what we had done with our *Heilig*, nor was he satisfied until I told him of the record with the composer's playing of it.

5*

Edward Heath tells us in his book of the excitement he had in playing for some of our finest artists. The excitement would not be one sided. No matter how eminent a violinist or 'cellist might be, he could hardly regard being accompanied by a Prime Minister as an everyday experience. Even Pablo Casals with quiet pleasure told me that he had been accompanied by Queen Victoria down at Osborne.

All the same I could not understand why Mr. Heath should be surprised that he had to jump four bars in a Handel Sonata when his violinist partner had a lapse of memory. Why, bless your heart, we professionals are the nimblest people in the world when it comes to skipping. We are adepts at jumping, as sure footed as mountain goats; for us there is no close season for jumping or steeplechasing.

I cannot resist while on this frisky subject, repeating a few sentences from my book *Am I too Loud?*

> Coenraad von Bos was accompanying Elena Gerhardt in Hugo Wolf's *Lied vom Winde* (Song of the Wind) when Elena omitted almost two pages in the middle of the song. Thanks to the pianist's adroitness the audience was unaware of this giant gap— well, they must have been unaware, for they clamoured for the song to be repeated. 'Won't they be bewildered,' whispered Bos to the singer before they restarted 'to find the song has become much longer.' In truth the first attack of wind had been a short one.

On a glorious July evening we went to Chequers to a birthday party for Mr. Heath who received us in the rose garden and remarked that we were near neighbours. This is true though I fancy our abode might if anything, be a little smaller. We sat with Clifford and Lucille Curzon and enjoyed a recital given by Gina Bachauer. When it was over Robert Armstrong, Mr. Heath's principal private secretary, called 'Prime Minister, will you wait for a moment' and we all kept our seats while a record was placed on the gramophone cabinet at the back of the music room. We were rewarded with no sound—some mechanical defect meant two or three minutes of silence—and I broke it by saying, 'Prime Minister, there is something wrong with your Cabinet,' which amused Messrs. Heath and Curzon though I cannot answer for the reaction of other Ministers of the Crown who were present. Eventually the music started. It was a tribute to our host organized by Sir Georg Solti; it began with *Alla bella Despinetta*, the sextet from *Così fan tutte*, followed by four singers who sang in different languages 'Happy birthday dear Ted' with a *finale* in English sung by the whole cast (they had been recording *Così*). The record was presented to the P.M. naming all the artists including the 'Accompanist on harpsichord, G. Solti'.

I am conscious that in this little effusion I have boasted to some extent of having sniffed the rarefied air of the corridors of power or, to put it more precisely, of having indulged in the autobiographer's prerogative of name dropping. At least I can say that I am a friend of Edward Heath, but if I were asked 'How friendly?' I would reply as politicians reply to a poser they cannot answer by saying, 'That is a leading question'. Let me answer it as Leslie Henson, the actor, answered John McCormack. John could be tediously aggressive in his cups. Having asked Henson if he knew Compton Mackenzie well and getting an affirmative reply, he persisted, 'But do you know Monty very very very well?' 'Only one very,' replied the actor impatiently, 'after all I am only bowling my hoop.'

Early Morning Tea

RUDOLF BING became one of the most celebrated impresarios of his time, running the Edinburgh Festival for a number of years before moving on to the Metropolitan Opera in New York, but it was at Glyndebourne that the seeds of his reputation were sown. He has a charming paragraph—among many others—in his *5,000 Nights at the Opera,** about his first visit to this enchanting place in the Sussex Downs. He was particularly impressed by Childs, John Christie's perfect butler and godfather to one of John's children.

> P. G. Wodehouse could have modelled Jeeves after him. Once in later years when I needed Christie for something and could not find him, I asked Childs where he was, and Childs told me; it was some entirely unexpected out-of-the-way place. 'Childs,' I said, 'how do you know he is *there*? Did you ask him before he left?' Childs said, 'A good butler never asks his master where he is going, but he always knows.' On one of the first occasions that I was an overnight guest at Glyndebourne, Childs woke me with that abominable English custom, the early-morning tea, and said, 'Breakfast at eight-thirty, sir.' I said, 'Good morning, Childs. What time is it now?' 'Nine o'clock, sir,' he said.

That abominable English custom! How I agree with Rudy Bing!

No matter what time of day I arrive at some provincial hotel, I find it irritating when I am signing the register to be greeted by the mechanical and stereotyped 'Will you be wanting early morning tea?'

It happened to me once after an all night journey. I had just 'signed in' and was proceeding straight to the breakfast room when the receptionist called, 'Will you be wanting etc. etc.' like an old record. I returned to the desk and asked, 'Do you want me to go up to my

---

* Hamish Hamilton, 1972.

bedroom and have it now?' She answered frigidly, 'Will you be
wanting it tomorrow morning?' By this time I had incurred her displeasure—I had deranged her routine with the result that an urgent
message regarding rehearsal arrangement waiting for me in her office
was disregarded. Two hours were wasted while I hung around waiting
for a telephone call from my colleague who naturally asked me,
'Didn't you get my message?' I did not explain that when I arrived, the
receptionist had been too worried about the morrow's tea—twenty-
four hours later.

No wonder the Mormons ban tea, but on occasion I almost understand them. The drinking of tea, coffee and other such stimulants is
prohibited in their creed: it follows inevitably that hard liquor, as it is
termed in America, is forbidden too but there are limits beyond which
my sympathy cannot extend. Several times I have lectured at the
Brigham Young University in Utah. The lecture is due to start at
eleven so I am called for in Salt Lake City fairly early and driven
through a fertile wide-sweeping valley to this Mormon seat of learning
in Provo, some thirty miles away. By the time we are nearing the
environs of the University I begin to get that 'elevenses' feeling so I
ask the young man who is driving if it is possible to have a cup of tea.
'Out of the question on our Campus,' he replies, 'it's against our
principles.' However, I did receive stimulation of a spiritual nature,
for the Principal led the audience in the vast auditorium in prayers that
I should be given strength and inspiration during the next hour to
deliver my message. I think it was extremely civil of him. A cup of tea
would not have come amiss.

Well, they are a wonderful audience and I have never seen a happier
crowd of young people. After all, there are compensations: what you
lose on the swings you gain on the roundabouts. And let's face it, a
cup of tea or a cup of coffee are all very well but they are not so much
fun as polygamy.

Many artists, myself included, dislike staying privately when fulfilling engagements even when their hosts are friends; in an hotel you
can order your meals, your drinks, take your rest or read, come and go,
as you please. Benno Moiseiwitsch the pianist, nearly had a fatal heart
attack when he was forced to accept the hospitality of a lady in the
north of England. It was during the war and all the hotel accommoda-
tion was fully booked. His hostess was a charming woman, but
massive, overwhelmingly and noisily enthusiastic and by no means
Benno's cup of tea. (Tea! There it is again.) At all events she burst into
his bedroom at eight the morning after his concert clad in an ill-fitting

dressing-gown bearing a tray. 'Your early morning tea,' she boomed triumphantly.

Benno told me afterwards that it was the biggest fright he had experienced during the whole course of the war.

Hymn of Praise

MY PURPOSE in this chapter is to present some of my favourite Schubert songs, they only qualify for inclusion by being virtually unknown or unjustifiably neglected. No mention will be made, in the fifty or more songs that follow of any of the well-known Goethe or amazing Heine settings (the Heine and Müller *Lieder* I attempted to deal with elsewhere*) or popular songs, such as *Die Forelle* (The Trout), *An die Musik* (To Music), *Frühlingsglaube* (Faith in Spring). Since the Mandyczewski Edition is something of a rarity I am setting down my collection according to the Peters Edition of which there are seven volumes.

Volume I.

Let us dismiss this treasure in a few words for it is known and loved by everyone. It embraces the three great cycles *Die Schöne Müllerin* (Maid of the Mill), *Winterreise* (Winter's Journey), and *Schwanengesang* (Swan Song), also thirty-four miscellaneous songs making a total of ninety-two. If Schubert had written none other than these we would worship him, but in the short space afforded him on this earth he still found time to write hundreds and hundreds more.

* * *

Volume II.

Meeres Stille (Sea Stillness) is a setting of Goethe composed in 1815. Not a breath of air ruffles the stillness of the grey waters, the boatman looks in vain for the merest ripple on the surface. All is quiet with a deadly foreboding of the coming storm.

Although the instruction is *Sehr Langsam* (very slowly) there are two not four beats to the bar; Schubert adds, for the singer's benefit, *ängstlich* (anxiously). The phrases are long and should be sung with almost expressionless smoothness, the atmosphere of breathless

* *The Schubert Song Cycles.*

suspense is nullified if the singer himself is breathless. Grace notes should be delivered unhurriedly. It is important for the first note in each bar of the vocal line to coincide with the last (top) note of the pianoforte's slowly spread chord. No *crescendo* is to be made with any rising phrase—all is uniformly *pp*.

Elena Gerhardt's performance of this *Lied* was memorable.

★   ★   ★

Am Strome (By the River) to Mayrhofer's words in another example of Schubert's love of water music. This time it is not rippling but flowing placidly to the sea. 'My life is reflected here,' muses the singer, 'I have had calm sunny stretches, have had floods of temper and dismal days and now like you, dear river, flowing to the ocean, I shall merge into the infinite.'

This charming song is in A,B,A form, the centre animated section suggests the playfulness of youth and later the trials that beset him—which are not to be taken too seriously or made too dramatic. True, there is an *ff* and an allusion to storms, but this need not be overdone because the prevailing mood is found in the two outer movements (Verses 1 and 3) with their quiet contented flow. It is reminiscent of Paul Bourget's *Beau Soir*, in Debussy's song

> Car nous nous en allons, comme s'en va cette onde
> Elle à la mer, nous au tombeau.

Mayrhofer says that happiness is not attainable on earth but Schubert thrusts such thoughts away and sees the sunlight's gleam on the water.

★   ★   ★

Der Schiffer (The Seaman). This boatman in Mayrhofer's verses likes to 'stand up to the tempest like a man'; let the waters rage impotently, 'soaked to the skin I am in my element and have no use for a life of comfort.'

I have little sympathy for these hearty gentry, though paradoxically I find the song enjoyable to play. By all means let the singer convince us that he relishes the sentiments expressed herein so long as the pianist is allowed to rattle away happily on his keyboard thanking his lucky stars he is on *terra firma*. *Der Schiffer* evokes enthusiastic response from the listeners.

★   ★   ★

Der Zwerg (The Dwarf) is a horror story by the same poet who wrote *Nacht und Träume*, Matthaus von Collin. The court dwarf takes his mistress, the queen, out to sea and after strangling her casts her body in the water because she has been unfaithful to him by co-habiting with her husband the king. They both weep before the dread deed, she seemingly recognizing that her infidelity merits such terrible retribution. As for the dwarf, who holds these singularly strange standards of morality—he was never seen again.

Despite the absurdity of the story, which we are told Schubert tossed off in no time, the music is gripping. A Beethovian figure of Fate (Fifth Symphony) is heard in the pianoforte bass; subservient to this nearly always, but never ceasing, are the palpitating semiquavers in the treble—these are true semiquavers but give the impression of *tremolo* by means of the sustaining pedal. The singer gives voice as if he were carried along on the black wings of the ominous opening bars. By maintaining a bodeful *pp* he controls the situation so that the sudden *sforzandi* are made the more startling, thus there is something in reserve for the climaxes. A big baritone voice is needed to do justice to these, and also a voice which can be reduced to a thread at such phrases as *da küsst der Zwerg die bleichen Wangen* (The dwarf kisses the pallid cheeks) and the final *An keiner Küste wird er je mehr landen* (On no coast will he ever set foot).

* * *

Mayrhofer's *Schlaflied* or *Schlummerlied* (Lullaby) has a similar and utterly Schubertian character that I find in *Die Sterne* (The Stars) (Leitner) and *Der liebliche Stern* (The Lovely Star) (Schulze), they each have a mesmeric quality, a heavenly monotony that holds you, makes you regretful when they are over. Here is Schubert in his beloved woodland, marvelling at the song of the stream, close to mother earth, cradled in complete relaxation by the sound and sight of nature. The *legato* lyrical line of the singer is delicately thrown in relief by the *pizzicato* chords (first right hand, then left) in the accompaniment. It is very softly sung throughout and if the listener is so entranced that his head nods—the singer should not feel too offended.

* * *

Nachtstück (Nocturne) again is Mayrhofer. We are told in an impressive and intentionally hesitant beginning that the moon contends with the mist on the mountains and it is very much in keeping if this is sung *quasi* recitative in style, that is, with an expressive freedom. But 'the old man takes his harp, wanders into the woods and softly sings' is at once self-possessed and firm, the mood resolute, preparing us in seven short bars for the glorious melody that now comes. It is a noble ample tune (if my good fairy allowed me a singing voice I should ask to sing this). 'O holy night soon I shall sleep the long sleep that will liberate me from all grief.' Over a flowing harp-like accompaniment the old man conjures the heavens in a voice that floats serenely and reverently; with softness, yes, but with a softness that is suggestive of undisclosed power. (The Alexander Kipnis quality.)

Let *der Alte* rest, the poem continues, and as the old one falls silent the rustling leaves of the trees supplant the harp for accompaniment, lulling him to his eternal sleep.

Richard Capell's only criticism of the song is its unconvincing poem otherwise he would put it among the finest of Schubert's songs. But I prefer, when my heart is clutched, to be more naive—and this is the only approach for the performer if he is to be convincing. To me this is a great song.

★ ★ ★

Normanns Gesang (Norman's Song). 'The heath this night shall be my bed,' from Scott's *Lady of the Lake* is one of those epics that extols the tiresome man of action glorying in clash of arms and slaughter but who finds time to dream of his return to the bride from whose side he was torn at the church door by the call of battle, and certain no doubt, that his Mary will wait with patient understanding for his triumphant return.

My distaste for the sentiments expressed in the song does not preclude it from this collection.

It has a fascination caused by its driving demoniacal energy. Without exception every bar has a jarring, urging, rhythm not the dainty tripping of a palfrey in single notes but the full-fisted chords of a war-horse. Occasional jolting *sforzandi* are thrown in for good measure.

There are seven pages of it (Peter's Edition) and the pianist is in danger of developing St. Vitus's dance in his right fore-arm unless he perceives (as in *Erlkönig* and *Auf der Bruck*) that there are plenty of *piano* signs.

The singer is glad of these signs too, for it means he can make his voice heard. The vocal line does not tie itself invariably to the pianoforte's pattern, there are anacruses in plenty for the voice and such passages as *Maria, Holde, sein* are exhilarating in their freedom from the accompaniment's iron-clad regularity.

★ ★ ★

Lied des gefangenen Jägers (Song of the Imprisoned Huntsman, from Walter Scott's *Lady of the Lake*). I do not for one moment claim this as vintage Schubert but it is a brave outburst, enjoyable to sing and play and is rousing for the listener. The singer will find little here to strain him—the vocal line is restricted to an octave's range—he must in consequence guard against the tendency to rant and rend the air above the boisterous accompaniment. His partner should help by exercising some discretion. In Polonaise rhythm throughout, it is too short to become tiresome. A recitalist ending a group with this energetic affair will not quit the stage to the sound of his own footsteps.

★ ★ ★

An den Mond (Holty): (To the Moon.) 'Unveil yourself, sweet moon, that your beams will reveal the trysting-place of former days. Alas, show me no more: the place is forsaken and I the forsaken one weep.'

Hearing the three-bar piano introduction is enough to tell us that we are in the presence of an exalted song. Although the mood is quiescent, the 'cello-like bass in the opening three bars of the pianoforte is to be played impressively; these bars should make an immediate impact for their air is never heard again.

As gently as a silver cloud, and as smoothly, the vocal line floats seemingly impervious to the singer's invocation. It seems aloof because it is so far removed, so high in the clef from the low bass in the accompaniment: the singer adds to this illusion by rejecting any idea of a *crescendo* on the three mounting crucial phrases *wo Phantasien und Traumgestalten* . . . etc. (Fantasies and dreams.) It is tempting to augment the volume in these moments and, of course, is much easier than maintaining the preferable *mezza voce*.

The song is in A-B-B-A form and it is in the two middle sections where the moon comes down to earth (if I may be forgiven the expression) that it unveils itself (*Enthülle dich*). These sections are *alla breve* and in contrast to the slow 12/8 of the main tune.

This tune now returns more sadly than formerly as the forsaken one begs to be left in darkness and in tears.

★ ★ ★

Dithyrambe (Schiller) calls for musical finesse and mastery of language. It is marked *Geschwind, feurig* (Quick, fiery) but is so full of *bonhomie* that *spirited* is a better description than *fiery*. A strophic three verse it is superb Schubert with lines and half lines of Schiller repeated to fill out the musical design.

'Never will the gods appear singly, never alone: no sooner had I welcomed Bacchus than Cupid appeared, even Phoebus descended from his heavenly throne. What can a man offer you, ye gods? O, pour out the nectar, hand me the cup.'

The five-bar introduction is decidedly Bacchic in gusto with rollicking *sforzandi* scattered liberally. Rhythm is the vital spark, the all-important element right through the song. It is exemplified in the penultimate bar of the prelude, here the pianist uses a tight reign, he holds back the impetuous rush (it is *rubato* rather than *rallentando*) only to let the *Geschwind* movement obtain in the last bar so as not to impede his partner's attack. It has to be done without loss of energy and is aggressively *staccato*. And attack us the singer does: *Nimmer das glaubt mir, erscheinen die Götter*: he shoots every word at us so that a listener who knows not one word of German can understand the drift of it. Perfect enunciation and masterly rhythmic control are the keys to the song's delivery. This authority is essential on the second page, for, to a *piano*, the singer has grace notes; these must be accommodated by holding back the tempo otherwise it is certain these grace notes will be clumsy and lose their joviality. Towards the end of each stanza the vocal line sinks down below the stave but the singer's spirit does not drop, this he must consciously avoid: here the pianist can help by not taking his instruction *forte* too literally.

★ ★ ★

Heimweh (Homesickness). Schubert set only one other Johann Pyrker poem to music besides this, *Die Allmacht*, but since this mighty song is known to everyone I am not dealing with it here. Certainly *Heimweh* is not up to that level but has some fine moments in its eight pages. It is in A,B,C,A form.

Torn from his native Alps, the exile droops like a withered flower says the first verse, and the disconsolate man's spirits seem to rise at the mere mention of his native mountains, only to fall away heavy-heartedly at the tail end of each phrase; twice Schubert repeats *entrissen dahin* (torn away) with emphasis. Section B sees a charming argument between the voice with its steady duple tempo and the piano's triplets; it is warming and pastoral as the singer pictures the hut where he was born, the green meadows and woods. But when he comes to describe his mountains 'towering peak upon peak' the music too mounts to a majestic *ff*. This climax is well prepared by a gradual and heartening *crescendo*. The piano's slender triplets first remarked early in verse two, developed into massive chords as we moved from meadow to mountain, but now we come to the most playful section of the song and the music changes character completely; it is a *Scherzo* in 3/4 time and in the tonic major. Schubert's 'effects' are an amusing feature, for to the words *Er höre das Muhen der Kühe* ('he hears the lowing of cattle') we have suddenly obtruding in the A major key a mooing F natural in the piano bass (the onomatopoeia of *Muhen* is to be recognized) and when the home-sick man hears in his imagination the shepherds and milkmaids yodelling, Schubert allows the pianist a veritable yodel.

The last section reverts to the pattern of the opening with its unfulfilled longing and its painfully re-iterated *unwiderstehlicher Sehnsucht*.

* * *

Auf der Bruck (Schulze): On the Bruck with its irresistible forward drive and the thudding hooves of the horse remind the pianist—as his wrist begins to feel the strain—of *Erlkönig* with its repetitive chords and octaves. The rider, however, has only one thought, to return to his sweetheart's side, so 'On, good horse, without delay through night and rain'. It goes without saying that the more difficult the accompaniment the quicker will the singer want to move and it must be allowed he has every reason, in this joyous ebullient song. However, he will find that though there are exhilarating outbursts in plenty, they will have greater impact by recognizing that much of the song (again like *Erlkönig*) remains *p* and *pp* and this he can use to advantage without losing one jot of his vitality. Clarity of enunciation in the bouncing vocal line will be helped by this treatment.

'Why falter?' asks the rider of his horse. It is a question the accompanist could answer readily. Actually the rapid repeated chords in the treble which bother him are, apart from the occasional *sforzandi*, lightly played and it is the canon-like bass coming so buoyantly a half bar after the voice that predominates.

* * *

Die Sterne (Leitner): (The Stars.) Again Schubert's genius casts its spell over us and the question arises 'How does he do it?' No other song writer can confound us by the utter simplicity with which he achieves such magic.

A pianist approaching *Die Sterne* for the first time will see four pages, uniform in pattern and rhythm, with a piano part in block harmony— but appearances with Schubert are sometimes deceptive. Listening to the floating *legato* of the singer's rising phrase *Wie blitzen die Sterne so hell durch die Nacht* (How brightly the stars sparkle in the darkness) and then the graceful descent *Bin oft schon darüber von Schlummer erwacht* (they often rouse me from sleep) a sensitive accompanist will note it is sung with lightness and smoothness; a delicate increase in tone is made as the line rises and a decrease as it declines. This is his clue. His tone becomes light and airy as his partner's—and as smooth. Careful use of the sustaining pedal is essential: too little of it will be disturbing and choppy, too much of it will create a blur making the singer's *hell* (bright) meaningless. Concentrated listening and experiment are involved.

I draw attention to the *turn* in the dominant seventh cadence which invariably comes two bars before the voice's entry in the introduction and interludes, it needs a little time allowance, to be effected with grace.

The singer finds the modulation from E flat (the tonic key) to C major comes so blandly that he takes it in his stride, but when the return to the home key comes, he draws our attention to it (*sie üben im stillen*, etc.) by giving the first syllable of *üben* a little stress in time and tone. A similar situation occurs after the enharmonic modulation to the relative major when he again returns to the tonic (*und tragen oft küsse*, etc.).

'May your sparkle, dear stars, ever be a blessing to me' is the burden of the poet's message.

Slight enough material but sufficient for Schubert to bewitch us.

* * *

Himmelsfunken (Heaven's Sparks). Silbert's is another evocation inspired by the stars and the soft night air. The heart drunk with ecstasy longs for the peace of heaven.

There is a fascinating ambiguity here; Schubert leads us to believe by the frequent appearance of F naturals at the song's beginning that C major is the home key and it is not until the last bars that we hear its base is G major. This is not only of academic interest, it shrouds the dear little song in mystery; it inspires the singer with a little awe. A charmed modulation to the remote key of B flat at *das trunkne Herz vergeht* (the drunken heart expiring) catches the heart as the voice ascends on *Herz*, as if the soul were truly uplifted. (The possibility of an unobtrusive *portamento* on this *Herz* should be considered but it is hardly to be recognized except by the singer himself—the listener will be affected but knows not why.)

It is sparse, it is simple, it is Schubert.

★ ★ ★

Volume III.

Memnon. Mayrhofer is obsessed as he was in *Nachtstück* to embrace eternal peace, unrealizable in this world. Here, however, although written two years earlier than *Nachtstück* Schubert reaches even greater heights.

A statue at Thebes, Egypt, of Amenoth III is thought to be that of Memnon, an Ethiopian king who fought on the Trojan side. Legend says that at sunrise it gives out a musical sound to greet his mother, Eos (the Dawn). 'I long to be united with thee, O Morning's Goddess, far from this world's emptiness and become a star—silent and pale' (*Ein stiller bleicher Stern*).

Never did a song need more intense concentration from singer and pianist than this. For their sake, and the listeners', one must *feel* the silence before starting the introduction. *Schwärmerisch* (visionary) is the instruction and although *sehr langsam* it is *alla breve*—a very slow two beats to the bar. It is the alto voice in this prelude which gradually impinges on the ear and is made impressive of necessity, because it has only one more appearance and is very beautiful. The triplet octaves are in parentheses. 'Breaking the eternal silence' the singer's entry is hushed but tone rises and warms as 'Aurora's purple rays pierce the enveloping mist'. Octaves in the accompaniment, once so subdued, now become a feature at an enharmonic change from the tonic (D flat) to F major and the music conveys with intention an impression of simulated felicity to the words 'My song seems inspired by happiness to the human ear.' The vocal line, without loss of smoothness, contributes to this illusion by its almost jaunty rhythm and exaggerated intervals (ninths). Yet the singer is careful to observe Schubert's *ppp* for this section is the calm before the passionate 'I, to whom Death beckons'. This is heralded by those octave triplets now in the bass, ever loudening.

No more divine music can be found in all Schubert than the last page of *Memnon*, it has returned to that purple key of D flat: over gentlest triplet quavers in the pianoforte, the singer's melody goes directly to your heart. This melody, as he prays to become *ein stiller bleicher Stern*, drops from heaven to earth and then rises again, in endearing intervals into which the singer puts all his love and tenderness. Heaven be praised, the phrase is repeated—it is almost too much to bear.

After this, the postlude becomes a profound responsibility. It must be treated very softly but still intensely and without too much regard for strictness of tempo.

*   *   *

Der Schäfer und der Reiter (Friedrich von Fouqué): (The Shepherd and the Knight.) A shepherd and his sweetheart, billing and cooing under the shadow of the beech trees, are disturbed by a knight clattering past: 'Come and sit with us; my darling will weave a garland of beautiful blooms for you,' calls the smiling rustic. 'Never,' replies the frowning horseman, 'I strive for glory and gold, not for easeful pleasures.'

Playful semiquavers in the vocal line and trilling birds in the piano-forte paint a pastoral scene rudely interrupted by the galloping rhythm, announcing the arrival of the warrior on the scene. Of course he sings in the minor mode (he would!) but the shepherd renews his invitation, this time in a higher—and again major—key. The rider, unfortunately, has the last word and we are left with him clattering off in dudgeon. I would rather have been left with the shepherd, or better still with his fair Chloe.

*   *   *

Ellen's zweiter Gesang (from Walter Scott's *Lady of the Lake*). Easily the finest setting from Scott is *Ave Maria* but it is too well known for inclusion here. I enter Ellen's second song for no other reason than my liking for it.

'Huntsman rest, thy chase is done.' Marked *etwas geschwind* (some-what quickly) it requires some stretch of the imagination to take it as a lullaby, for, paradoxically, it is a most lively affair. Hunting horns abound but must surely be muted, yet it is full of Schubertian *joie de vivre*. Singer and partner perform it with relish—remembering it is nearly all *pp*; their enjoyment will be infectious.

*   *   *

Dass sie hier gewesen (Rückert) is one of Schubert's precious jewels, it is short, in strophic form with three quatrains. 'That there is fragrance in the air proves that you were here.' Not until the last line of the verse, *Dass sie hier gewesen*, do we conclusively reach the home key; Schubert reveals it in concert with the poet. Music and words converge after the tender ambiguity.

Soft discords from the piano introduce the detached sighs of the singer; both artists observe all the silences (rests) and yet an over-all feeling of smoothness prevails. This can be achieved by the singer who does not regard a *rest* as synonymous with a breath—if he can possibly cover his first seven bars without breathing, so much the better, but should this be beyond him at this slow tempo, he must breathe unostentatiously. If a breath is necessary in bar fourteen after the semiquaver (and correspondingly in the other verses) it is unhurried; everything comes willingly to a standstill while it is being taken.

This is as loving a compliment for the adored one as can be paid by a man, but women sing it occasionally. It was a favourite with Elisabeth Schumann.

★ ★ ★

Das Zügenglöcklein (Seidl). The passing bell (the octave in the treble) is heard in almost every bar; for all that, it is the alto voice which predominates in all the solo piano sections. The music alternates between the major and the minor—a beguiling practice of our Schubert—*Die Götter Griechenlands* for instance, though here the mood is far less tortured. It can be called a strophic song but each verse differs a little from its neighbour.

While finding it rewarding to perform, the accomplished singer will not find it taxing. Cool, lyrical singing is needed, there is little that is mournful in it for the bell's tolling does not inspire gloom and ends with the invocation 'Call him to you, O Lord, if you will, but if there is still friendship and love for him grant him a further stay in this dear world of ours.'

★ ★ ★

Im Walde (In the Forest). Schubert seizes the poem as he did Schulze's *Auf der Bruck* and drives it on relentlessly. It was written two years before *Erstarrung* (Numbed) and foreshadows that marvellous creation not only with its restless triplets but, rather less masterfully, in his handling of the text.

The introduction is all agitation with aching passages in the treble.

Impelled by the urge that drives his affinity in *Wegweiser* (The Sign Post) (*Winterreise*) the wanderer's complaint 'Woe attends me and never leaves me' is keenly expressed in the desperately reiterated G flats. He tramples on the wild flowers, he shuts his ears to the birds. When will he find rest?

Since the music repeats itself with the main subject coming four times and a secondary tune twice, it is imperative to move at a quick pace though the composer says 'Not too quick'. But in Peters there are nine pages and the singers should not prolong them.

It is well worth listening to Fischer-Dieskau on his record where he manages to give us a *legato* line in contrast to the restless accompaniment and it is to be noted how he takes advantage of the stretches where Schubert asks for *piano*: unadulterated *forte* does not obtain throughout.

★ ★ ★

Wiegenlied. As in Seidl's *Das Zügenglöcklein* Schubert puts the poet's lullaby into the key of A flat. The song was one of Elena Gerhardt's favourites and because of this became one of mine. Like the enchanting *Das Lied im Grünen* (Song of Green) it goes on too long and the third verse (*Wie des Gelockes*, etc.) is usually omitted; the composer, we can be fairly certain, would not have objected.

The lulling melody at first has a series of one-bar phrases—each a descending curve—a soft hand gently closing a babe's eyelids; to the words 'Close your eyes so', come more extended two-bar phrases. The temptation to make a *crescendo* on a rising passage should be avoided; true it is asked for occasionally but even then is but a slight nuance.

★ ★ ★

Viola (Schober). In writing this title I can almost hear the groans of those of my readers who are acquainted with (but possibly have not heard!) this song—sixteen pages and over nineteen minutes in length. Capell complains it is like unto an horticultural show; no single flower he contends, should claim our attention for so long. Schubert did indeed indulge in some overlong extravagances, trying even to the most rabid Schubertian; I shall be alluding to one or two of them in my next chapter. *Viola* broadly, can be said to consist of three spun-out songs rolled into one, but each section contains vocal and piano writing of great beauty. The trouble with long effusions is that they lose shape—they sprawl—with one section bearing no relation to another.

I do not feel this criticism is fair with *Viola* for it is in *Rondo* form (very freely I admit) with a cohesion between the various movements: often the motif in the pianoforte, the little snow-bell (*Schneeglöckchen* or Snowdrop) wanders intriguingly from one section to another. It is full of invention, redolent of Schubert's love of nature and never sags on any page; eternally fresh. Look, for instance, at the second verse *Denn du kündest frohe Zeit* (You presage a happy time) how joyful it is! But my favourite moment of all is the singer's *Rose nahet, Lilie schwankt* (The rose approaches, lilies wave) and the preceding four bars of pianoforte interlude are melting in their loveliness.

Fischer-Dieskau recorded this with me but I only remember performing it once in public with a fine English artist, Astra Desmond.

★ ★ ★

Der liebliche Stern. Schubert set nine poems of Schulze the best loved of them being *Im Frühling* (In Spring). 'The Lovely Star', however, is another instance where the composer's love of nature casts a spell, on me at least.

Der Busen so bang und schwer, the poet's plaint that his heart is heavy when he beholds the stars, is not taken too seriously by Schubert who, while admittedly allowing the music here to drift into the minor, expresses himself with wistfulness rather than melancholy. He sees the stars' dancing reflection in the water and is more aware of the soft breeze of spring.

Marked *Etwas langsam* (somewhat slowly) I find the 'somewhat' misleading. Certainly there are two beats to the bar but if they are not slow beats the intrinsic charm of the music is lost. Over an *ostinato* figure in the accompaniment the vocal line must be very very *legato* with the telling semiquavers pressed out—lingered on—as much as the singer dares without distorting the rhythm. Although no indication is given and the melodic line *appears* restless it calls for the smoothest delivery and the earnestness and quality of tone that the singer would use in Caccini's *Amarylli*. This treatment makes *Es zittert von Frühlings-winden* (Airs of Spring) and *manch Sternlein sah ich entblüh'n* (I saw many a starlet's birth) bring tears to my eyes—but not if the singer does not love each phrase; not if the tempo is too fast; not if the smoothest calmest line is pitched away.

At a leisurely pace the accompanist is enabled to let us hear the occasional pair of *staccato* semiquavers which add piquancy to the rhythmic pulse.

I have heard the song dismissed as humdrum and it can easily become so. Mark Raphael's performance of it (he is a descendant, musically speaking, of Raymond von zur Mühlen) still lingers in my memory and I have had a warm affection for it ever since.

★ ★ ★

Aus Heliopolis (Mayrhofer). A wild prospect of rocks, cascades, sweeping winds of unimaginable power. The picture is allegorical and points the moral that courage is required to cleanse the mind of dross, to find an answer to life's enigma.

Quick and powerful, it is a brave song for a bass. For the pianist the dashing semiquavers in unison or alternating between the two hands add momentum to the mighty swinging rhythm, but he takes care that his booming bass, moving in conjunction with the vocal line does not submerge the singer. *Athme du dem heil'gen Aether, schling' die Arme um die Welt* (Breathe the blessed air, embrace the world) are phrases low in *tessitura* for the voice and the player must be merciful.

An evocation of violence and unremitting energy undoubtedly—but there are moments where a *piano* sign makes an appearance; it is to be observed. So should the rests in the pianoforte prelude, their slight prolongation adds muscle to the music.

★ ★ ★

Versunken (Goethe). At first sight the song looks as fierce as the preceding *Heliopolis* but in actuality is extremely playful. It goes like the wind and is one of Goethe's high-spirited trifles. The literal meaning of the title is 'Lost' but a more apt translation might be 'Enraptured'.

Comparing his hand to a five-toothed comb the fond admirer runs his fingers again and again through the curly locks of the pretty child; and before repeating the delicious caressing he kisses her brow, her eyes, her mouth. Her mouth? Then it is not a little child he is fondling! Perhaps it is Mme. Marianne von—but no, it is not my purpose to pry into the private affairs of Wolfgang von Goethe. At all events the singer can launch himself enthusiastically on the song with the comfortable feeling that all is above board though it seems to spell ruin to the *coiffure* of the maiden.

The tenor will find a soaring line with high notes on which he has time to expand, and the pianist a descriptive semiquaver figure in the treble to be treated with light—one might say caressing fingers.

* * *

Das Mädchen (Schlegel). This page of music could have been written by no other composer.

Despite her lover's protestations the girl has moments of uncertainty, wondering if his heart is true—and then—moments of contentment. Perhaps the nightingale can put her doubts to rest.

Again we have the Schubertian finger-print of major, minor, major.

In the vocal line gentle triplets are a feature of the song. Should the pianoforte's demi-semiquavers (thirty seconds) coincide with the last note of the singer's triplet? Decidedly they should. If they came just *after* (as they appear on the score) they would jolt the quietude of the maiden's meditation.

By divorcing the chord from the triplet a disturbance is created and this is as it should be *under stress*, as in the suffering of *Wasser-fluth* (Flood) or the strain of *Der Atlas*.*

* * *

Volume IV.

Auf der Donau (On the Danube). More picturesque regard to the sombre aspects of the poem (Mayrhofer) is paid here where they were blithely ignored in *Der liebliche Stern*. The boat glides past ruined castles, overgrown with weed and bracken; only undergrowth to be seen where towers and ramparts once proudly stood. The spirit sinks when contemplating the inexorable, lethal advance of decay. At first the singer has eyes only for the majestic ruins; under his quiet tune the even swing of the oar can be felt but he is soon disturbed by the ghostly rustle of fir trees. (The piano's *tremolo* is later followed by syncopation with sinister trills low in the bass.) Thrice he sings *Untergang* (sinking) with hushed awe and beneath him in the depths the accompaniment sinks chromatically down, down.

Beginning in E flat the music goes to F sharp minor where the song ends.

* * *

---

* *The Schubert Song Cycles.*

Wie Ulfru fischt (Mayrhofer): (Ulfru Fishing.) *Die Forelle* where the
angler caught his trout and *Fischerweise* (Fisherman's Song) where the
fisherman was too wily to be hooked by the girl's sly glances, both
overshadow *Ulfru*. But it is a fine blustery song, in the minor, with
some frustration expressed by the angler that the rod after bending and
twitching pulls nothing out. This exasperation is endorsed by the
pianoforte at the tail-end of each verse, though with more gusto than
ill humour. It is well worthy of a baritone's attention.

* * *

Selige Welt (Happy World). Originally composed for bass voice as was
Wie Ulfru fischt this song is reminiscent of *Heliopolis II*.

'Tossed on life's sea I do not steer my barque seeking like a fool some
Utopian isle of the blest: my landing place will be wherever I am cast
ashore.'

Let the pianist, when playing in unison with the voice, keep to a
lower dynamic level; he may crash to his heart's content when his
partner is tacit.

* * *

Der Alpenjäger (The Huntsman). This Schiller song is condemned out
of hand by most musicologists for its structure and the unmanageable
shape of the poem. There are three strophic verses where the mother
begs her son to attend the sheep; four more strophes where the boy—
now hunter—pursues and corners the trembling gazelle. The two
sections are separate worlds—two different songs—with music from
one bearing no relation whatsoever to the other and this is why the
pundits complain. But alas, the offence is compounded for suddenly a
ghostly figure appears from nowhere: it is the god of the mountains
come to protect the victim. 'Must you bring death and grief to my
herd?' he asks, and there the song ends with a page of undistinguished
music.

Much as I sympathize with the frightened animal and its tender eyes
I could have done without the spectral visitor; he ruins the song.

Why then do I include *Der Alpenjäger* in this collection? Because I
am captivated (not too strong an expression) by the tune the mother
sings. It has so much in it—so very much—that I love about Schubert,
a supplicating pliable melody abounding with melting *melisma* (i.e.
two or more notes sung to one syllable) and eloquent triplets pleading

against the piano's duple rhythm. The accompaniment resonantly supports the lovely tracery of the voice.

Mutter, Mutter lass mich gehen (Mother, let me go) from the boy comes in with startling effect and, not illogically, is more than twice the speed of the mother's pleading. This formula in 2/4 time covers the first three verses—after which my beloved C major tune is never heard again.

With four verses ahead of us occupied by the chase we leap off at full speed in a sudden transition to A flat. There must be no slackening of speed between the verses—it is fine and is exhilarating but it is a different composition.

We shall be forgiven if we do not linger too long over the last page. It was with Hermann Prey that I began to appreciate what beauty there is in the song and his voice is of a piece with the unforgettable tune and with the masculinity of the hunter.

★ ★ ★

An die untergehende Sonne (To the Setting Sun). Most of the Kosegarten verses were the composer's media in his formative years; not until 1816 do we find a song from this source that is really memorable and then came this setting and a beautiful one too; the last from Kosegarten.

It is a salutation to the sinking sun. In describing it as uneventful I imply that the even tenor of its way is undisturbed by startling modulations or changes of mood. The main tune comes thrice separated in true rondo form by two episodes; ever tranquil and lyrical and of true Schubertian vintage. *Immer tiefer, immer leiser, immer ernster, feirlicher* (Ever deeper, ever more softly, ever more earnestly, more solemnly). One can imagine by the metrical structure of the words how our composer would respond. It is a singer's song and I hear echoes of Janet Baker (those clear pure tones) singing *Die Nachtigall flötet dir Schlummergesang* (the nightingale's flute lulls you to slumber).

★ ★ ★

Der Schmetterling (Schlegel). The butterfly tastes the blossoms, defying you to protect them, he hovers and flits joyfully wherever caprice takes him. A short life for him and a happy one—and this goes for the song as well.

After the introduction high in the treble—so playful and flighty—

the piano descends at the voice's entry to a more resonant register. Since the singer will wish to sing as lightly as maybe, the pianist takes especial care that his bass fifths and octaves are featherweight; too much sustaining pedal makes them boom unpleasantly. Apart from the prelude, the score looks rather square and 'un-butterflyish', it is up to the pianist to keep it in the picture.

★ ★ ★

Der Wanderer (Schlegel). Not to be confused with the famous setting to Schmidt's words, this is a haunting song too refined and wistful to rival the other in popular favour but does not deserve to be abandoned.

'Keep moving as I do and trouble will not overtake you: this was the advice the moon gave me and I followed it. I am lonely but the world seems good to me.' *Wie deutlich des Mondes Licht zu mir spricht* is a cool and slender vocal line and does indeed suggest the floating moon high above. As if to remind the moon-gazer that one foot remains planted here below, the piano moves in unison with the voice. The same melody is repeated in the second verse, still very softly and pensively.

★ ★ ★

An die Laute (Rochlitz). This song is a little peach. One is reminded perhaps of Don Giovanni's Serenade *Deh, vieni alla finestra, o mio tesoro* (Come to the window my treasure) only because Mozart and Schubert both chose D major for their key and employed a similar lilting rhythm. That in each instance a plucked instrument is used is hardly a coincidence for your practised serenader has no other way to accompany himself. The means whereby both composers obtain their delicious effects are slender though in Schubert's case they are more rustic—and rightly so for his swain lacks the boldness and suavity of the licentious Don.

One unusual aspect of this song is worthy of notice; not one single word is addressed to the inamorata but, as the title says, to the lute. 'Softer, softer little lute.' Secrecy is the song's chief concern, its gist is to keep the neighbours ignorant of the serenader's prowess as a singer.

Yes, it is *pianissimo* throughout, but nevertheless it must exude vivacity. The words are projected with vigour but with minute singing tone—sung, as near as maybe, in a whisper; listeners will hear the words but only just catch the tune. Consonants (the sibilants in *leiser, flüstre,*

Fenster for instance) are clearly heard. In the last vocal phrase 'Nach-barn aber Nachbarn nicht (not my neighbours)—the final 'T' of *nicht* is made plain to all—I almost said displayed.

A word of advice to the singer: *An die Laute* is not recommended for a song recital in the Royal Albert Hall.

* * *

Hoffnung (Hope). In Schiller's *Der Alpenjäger* the vocal line seems to be borne out of the piano introduction so intimate is the intertwining of voice and accompaniment. Poetically it is poles apart from Schiller's *Hoffnung* but again I find here the closely woven texture that moves me in so much of Schubert's music.

The melody is free and sweeping in a swinging 6/8 time and the piano in block harmony clings to it all through; not playing in unison but underlining the turns of direction the voice takes. *Doch der Mensch hofft immer Verbesserung* (Yet man ever hopes for better days) is a fine rising phrase, increasing in volume the higher it mounts. As the voice ascends, the bass in the accompaniment descends step by step corres-pondingly. The goal is reached simultaneously, the singer on his ringing summit, the pianist on his resonant bass: it is a matter of seven bars and the culmination is rich and satisfying. Being a strophic song this generous phrase can be heard three times and it is particularly apt in the last verse to the words *Und was die innere Stimme spricht, das täuscht die hoffende Seele nicht*. (What the inner voice tells us will not disappoint the hopeful heart.)

* * *

An die Nachtigall (Claudius). The nightingale's song is brief here but with these few bars the soprano can touch our hearts if she is able to produce a tone of transparent clearness and purity. 'Love lies sleeping' says the maiden in a dreaming tempo—and at once it is the signal for the nightingale to chirrup sweetly in the pianoforte. *Nachtigall, ach, Nachtigall, ach!* is sung in melting entreaty (now in the minor). 'Do not inflame me with thoughts of love' vibrates with latent passion without losing its maiden meditation.

It is hoped the accompanist will observe the piquant *pizzicato* bass in the last bar of his introduction and in the first bar (treble) of his postlude.

* * *

Die vier Weltalter (Schiller): (The Four Ages of the World.)

Richard Capell's suspicion that Schubert was slightly mesmerized by the aura surrounding Schiller is borne out by the marathon odes *Der Taucher* (The Diver) and *Die Bürgschaft* (The Bond) he attempted, not invariably successfully, to put to music.

Here, man's acts (being *not* in seven ages) are made in twelve stages or verses ranging from conviviality to husbandry, to heroics and at last to minstrelsy. The composer had the good sense in this instance not to make a written-out song of it with different movements occupying twenty or more pages but to condense it to the strophic form, thus enabling the singer to excise a few verses, for refreshing though the music is it cannot be repeated a dozen times. Fischer-Dieskau sings verses 1, 6, 7, 8 only. In such a shortened history we may feel brief life is here our portion but at any rate it will be quite delightful.

★ ★ ★

Volume V.

Abendröthe (Sunset). Schubert wrote many salutations to the setting sun, they are for the most part miniatures, two exceptions are Kosegarten's *An die untergehende Sonne* and *Abendröthe* to Schlegel's words and this last is by far the finer of the two.

As if the glow of the sinking sun were veiled by a cloud the first bar is low in the bass, but the trill (trills are featured in the accompaniment throughout the song) gives promise of but a temporary shadow and a smiling mood; these are realized by the emergence in the treble of a ray of sunlight in a passage of reassuring tranquillity.

There is great beauty in the first seven bars of the score, but this is only the introduction, for the voice adds more magic to the scene. 'Deeper sinks the sun, the air is still and quiet' is sung to a celestial tune placed in a high register in marked contrast to the accompaniment. At *Tages Arbeit ist vollendet* (Day's work is done) the singer will be helped to thicken his tone slightly by the impression of toiling (but still *pp* and *legato*) in the piano part: this is important for his next phrase is light and airy, 'the children are at play', where the accompanist's trills are heard for the first time in the treble, fluting cheerfully. (My expressions 'thicken the tone' and 'light and airy' are dangerous suggestions if taken too literally, for all these distinctions in nuance and colour are to be made with subtlety and refinement, not pasted on with a thick brush.)

The texture is indeed less delicate at 'Mountains towering heaven-wards' with the trills again in the piano's bass. But with Schubert responding as ever to 'The great silvery stream' and with the pianist trying as much as he can to make his bass trills *pp* (very difficult because it is *legato* and needs sustaining pedal) the singer with his glorious sweeping phrases soars above everything.

The contemplation of the birds, distant people, mountains, winding stream (*Alles scheint dem Dichter redend*—all seem to speak to the poet), becomes a hymn of thanksgiving and is the emotional culmination.

Blessed with a voice and a sensitivity to do justice to this music, the singer will be able to pour a full heart into these lines for he has indeed cause to be thankful.

* * *

Am See (Bruchmann): (On the Lake.) In this little barcarolle Schubert takes a two-verse lyric and turns what might have been a fragment into a song. The first verse occupies only nine bars but the song is by no means half over for, without our being aware of any manipulation, the second verse lasts for twenty bars.

Over a soft *arpeggiando* accompaniment the singer's *legato* line moves placidly provided he avoids the tiresome habit of accenting the first beat of each bar.

We should not be allowed to know when he breathes; *Sonnenschein Sterne* (bars 8 and 9) are joined, for the arch on these words is spoiled by a breath, it can be taken after *Sterne. Himmels Pforten Sterne* in the second stanza is also linked; the words are the centre piece of a continuous train of thought 'There fall from heaven's gates stars, oh, so many stars.' *Viele* (many) is reiterated with the tone interrupted between each *viele*—and again the singer holds the thought by not breathing during these silences.

* * *

Dem Unendlichen (Klopstock): (To Infinity.) With this mighty *Te Deum* Schubert as in *Die Allmacht* (The Almighty) gives his pianoforte the role of the great organ with its majestic echoing chords and its thirty-two-foot diapason. It is an imposing introduction to a recitative of declamation never excelled in any other Schubert song: 'How the heart is exalted when it contemplates You, O Infinite One.' Like a bugle call 'Alone you call me from my night' leads from darkness to light culminating in a thrilling outburst 'Lord God of Hosts no hymn (*kein Jubel*) can adequately praise thee.'

The singer obeys no rigorous beat in this dramatic section, he responds to the impulsion of words and music and allows his high climax on *Jubel* to resound in the cathedral.

'Rustle, trees of life, to the harps' reverberation' is (to use an operatic term) the aria, it has a sweeping melody ranging from a low B flat to a high G flat and the pianist, although playing with a hundred harps and a powerful bass, listens carefully when the *tessitura* of the vocal line drops. 'Your harps resound' is a phrase that calls for a steady increase in tone to correspond with the climb in the vocal line, but the singer will be making a misjudgement if he takes *lispelt* (whisper) too literally: his norm should never drop below a *mezzo forte*.

The final *fortissimo Gott! Gott! Gott! ist es* (each time higher and louder) is followed by a startling silence of one beat; this silence should be slightly prolonged so that the following *den* explodes. The two partners hit the word *den*—the singer on his consonant, the pianist on his octave bass—with thunderous unanimity.

It would be a pity if the postlude poured cold water on the fire of exultation; the pianist should only allow it to be subdued by gradual degrees but the fervour must never be lost.

★ ★ ★

Von Mitleiden Maria (Schlegel): (Of Mary's Suffering.)
Schubert reached sublime heights in some of his religious settings (*Litanei, Die Allmacht, Dem Unendlichen*) but this is the only song where the crucifixion or rather the vigil of Mary on Calvary is the theme.

It is all in three-part writing, the last word in grief and exhaustion. The composer sees only stark reality and does nothing to mitigate it.

When in Paris I sometimes visit a convent to hear the nuns singing their offices. The disembodied quality of their voices, devoted but colourless, is strangely moving, and I have been drawn again and again to listen. Perhaps in this song some such thought could be followed by the singer to give an impression of unsubstantiality—almost as if in a trance.

The third verse can be omitted.

★ ★ ★

Der entsühnte Orest (Mayrhofer): (Orestes Purified.)
This song can be called a continuation of *Orest auf Tauris* but it can be sung by itself and is far more distinguished.

Gratitude to the gods for the mercy vouchsafed him washes the soul of the King of Mycenae as the gentle sea of his own land laps his feet.

Sins and bloodshed have been purged as he begs Diana leave to join his ancestors.

In the first two stanzas the deep waters softly roll in the accompaniment and the words (at first) are addressed to them in solemn phrases. (Schubert's *Sehr langsam* is mandatory: the semiquavers—wave upon wave—deceive the eye and must move very slowly.)

'My little boat is steered by waves of love' is less solemn and can be treated softly over an accompaniment which now has reduced its impressive swell to pleasing ripples.

All motion ceases at the arrival of Diana—'O you who saved me listen to my prayer' is for the singer as free in style as he can possibly make it between the pianoforte's solemn chords. (*Erhöre du mein Fleh'n—wurde—zu meinen* are instances where the pianist simply waits, allowing his partner all the time he wants.)

* * *

Freiwilliges Versinken (Mayrhofer): (Voluntary Retreat.)

Wohin, o Helios? Wohin? This question addressed to the sinking sun is preceded by two confident introductory bars which are quietly repeated when the voice with more constraint makes its appeal.

'My flaming body is immersed in the cool sea, let the pale moon succeed me while I depart in glory.'

It was suggested in the previous song that the singer without disturbing the rhythmic shape of the music should endeavour to impart some freedom to his declamation, he will find this can be achieved with more facility here where movement is slow and majestic. This applies particularly at *Ich nehme nicht, ich pflege nur zu geben* ('I do not take; my mission is to give') and thereafter. It is free and verges on the recitative. We are hardly conscious of motion, and feel the diminution of the sun's warmth and the coming of night by the shivering demi-semi-quavers (thirty-seconds) which are heard in the singer's first two phrases and later imitated in the accompaniment.

Wenn ich auf die Berge meine Krone lege (When I lay my crown on the mountain tops) are glorious moments with spacious falls of ninths on *Krone* and on *lege*.

This song is unique in all Schubert. He had certainly never written anything like it previously. Capell considers it carries a hint of *Der Doppelgänger* written eight years after.

* * *

Abendstern (Mayrhofer): (Star of Eve.)

'Why so aloof, lovely star, from your resplendent brethren?'

'I am love's obedient star.'

'Since you are Love's symbol, join them.'

'No. I sow but sorrowfully and never see the fruit of my sowing.'

Undeniably the evening star shines in splendid isolation but the suggestion that the star will not unite with his fellows because he himself is Love seems an abstruse explanation. If Mayrhofer's meaning is vague, Schubert's is transparent.

This is a sweet little song. The questions are set in the minor key but the star's answers—only faintly heard—are in the major.

Only *look* at the music, dear reader, and you will hear the dulcet tones of Janet Baker.

* * *

Der Winterabend (Leitner): (Winter Evening.)

> From my warm room I gaze out at the village, the snow has laid a blanket on it, muffling all its noise. Day is done, all is quiet and my only visitor is the moon. I sit in silence and my mind goes back to bygone moments of pure bliss. I sit and sigh in the silence, thinking, thinking.

Throughout the song the vocal line must be pliable, it bends and sways to accord appreciative regard to the main tune which is a melting melody. Semiquaver curves and 'turns' (mordents) are frequent and in all these the flowing tempo is gently restrained without in any way impairing smoothness. (It is, in fact, a hold-back in order to preserve smoothness.) The pianist in his introduction and interludes imitates the voice in his handling of these and tries to acquit himself as gracefully as the singer.

In Peters Edition there are six pages of music, let it be confessed the middle pages (3 and 4) are uninspired, but the others are pure Schubert and are so lovely that they carry the sagging centre-piece. When he sings *Denk' an Sie, an das Glück der Minne, seufzer still und sinne* (thinking of the bliss of pure love) Schubert, thank God, repeats it again and again with ever increasing sweet nostalgia. 'And thinking, thinking' is murmured (almost parenthetically) which is the secret of its tender and moving charm as an *obligato* to the pianoforte's song without words.

* * *

Auflösung (Mayrhofer): (Dissolution.)

'Sun, hide yourself: Sound be silent, and you Springtime, begone and let me be alone for I am held entranced by heavenly song. Depart, oh world! Never disturb these ethereal choirs.'

This outline, it is hoped, gives a slight idea of the frenzy which took possession of the poet. It is a state of morbid ecstasy not for one moment to be entertained by Schubert, in whose heart Spring was eternal, ever filled with the wonder of it. Even in *Die Taubenpost* (The Pigeon Post) the last notes he put to manuscript, the burden of the song is youth ever yearning for love and life. Mayrhofer's death wish is not reflected by Franz Schubert's music; the most inspired of all mortal singers transfigures it into an especial ecstasy of his own, carrying his own banner of delight and thankfulness for being alive.

It is glorious for the singer and makes great demands on him for the vocal line soars high and low in giant sweeps, where there is every reason to louden the tone irresistibly as the voice mounts. *Denn die Gluthen der Wonne versengen mein Gebein* (For the fires of bliss burn me to the marrow) is a huge five-bar phrase to be contained in one breath. Every opportunity should be seized to decrease the tone when it is logical to do so; for instance the very first entry *Verbirg dich Sonne* is *piano* over the accompanist's *pp*. *Die süssen ätherischen Chöre* must be given ringing top Gs and As. The ending *geh' unter, Welt* low in the voice, and a rumbling accompaniment with the left hand deep in the bass and the right hand unusually high (for Schubert) in the treble, contrive to make an unearthly ending to this masterpiece.

Even a most conscientious artist in some of the *melismata* (and particularly when he augments his tone) is guilty of introducing intrusive Hs and the vigilant pianist tells his partner when they make their unwelcome appearance.

* * *

Volume VI.

Die Einsiedelei (Salis): (The Hermitage.)

'By a purling spring almost hidden in the thicket I make a little grotto where I sit quietly in the shade, one with nature.'

The ceaseless rippling triplets of the pianoforte are really the winning feature here. There is no haste, the tempo is *moderato* and care is taken to maintain smoothness without losing the joyous bubbling of the fresh spring waters. Although Schubert did not 'go to town' over the voice part we must hear what the singer says. The accompaniment is always a trickle not a flood.

It is enough to sing verses one and three only. It is an improvement
to play the introduction again as an interlude between the verses.

* * *

Die Götter Griechenlands (Schiller): (The Gods of Greece.)
    A fragment from a very long and elaborate lyric, it is in honour of
the divinities of the ancients and is saturated by a hopeless, consuming
longing for the golden age.
    The pianist does well if he can match the voice's *legato* line, for his
accompaniment is mostly in block harmony and can jar if it does not
glide perfectly with the voice. Only in the middle of the song, the
minor section, does the piano have an individuality of its own where
the treble (against a harp-like plucking in the bass and played without
pedal) has a fluting counter melody. This song was discussed in more
detail in the chapter on Janet Baker.

* * *

Zum Punsche (Mayrhofer): (On Drinking Punch.)

    A merry heart goes all the day
    Your sad tires in a mile-a.

'My soul is merry indeed,' says the poet, 'when in cheerful company,
cups full of punch make the round. The waves are engulfing me, I am
no longer on firm ground; life's burden is cast off and I float on the
high seas of contentment.'
    If Peter Brueghel had an intimate perception of the Flemish peasant's
character, so Schubert could match in music what the other transmitted to canvas.
    This is to be sung with rustic gusto. No airs or graces here, we are
tossing off punch by the goblet not rolling vintage Burgundy or
Bordeaux round the palate with knowing nods and winks.
    The singer is always *forte*, he attempts to slake his enviably insatiable
thirst during the pianoforte interludes and only here is the accompaniment reduced in tone. We finish abruptly—without *rallentando*: that
final chord is the empty cup being banged on the board and demanding
attention.

* * *

Die Vögel (Schlegel): (The Birds.)

'What joy it is to flutter and sing, to look down from on high on these foolish mortals who are unable to fly. We get our fill of their choice fruit and twitter mockingly at their clumsy efforts to catch us.'

This song is particularly suitable for a light soprano where a deep contralto or bass would hardly sound air-borne. Chirruping semi-quavers abound and are as clear and clean as the notes of a bird. *Zu schweben, zu singen* (to hover and sing), *singen* is sustained and can be allowed an exultant little *crescendo*. But *Die Menschen sind töricht, Sie können nicht fliegen* (Men are foolish, they cannot fly) is heavier in texture (plodding fifths in the pianoforte bass) and *fliegen* has a short, impotent top note. The parallel phrase to this is *Wir flattern gen Himmel* (we fly up in the sky) and perhaps an extra beat on the G sharp of *Himmel* will emphasize our superiority.

Früchte wir pickten and *Beute gewinnen* (get our loot) are points where the singer can give verve and relish by holding the first syllables of *Früchte* and *Beute* as long as she dares (inevitably shortening the second syllable of each word). This adds a little gusto to the rhythm.

Double-stopping (to use a string player's term) occurs here and there in the accompaniment and needs practising for it must sound smooth and as easy as easy.

* * *

Die Blumenspracher (Platner): (The Language of Flowers.)

The flowers swaying in the summer breeze whisper confidentially of love.

This *billet doux* must have been dashed off in next to no time, it burgeons with the instinctive art that Alfred Brendel had in mind when he said, 'Schubert could write in his sleep,' for it is unaffected and uncomplicated.

Each verse (the song is in A.B.A. form) is a sestet divided into three phrases; two of seven bars and one of fourteen, and if the latter can be contained in one breath, so much the better. The vocal line bends and sways as gracefully as the blossoms, while the gently flowing triplets in the accompaniment, so dear to the composer's heart, add to the charm of the picture.

Since this song is rarely heard in public (the writer has only heard it in the Fischer-Dieskau Schubert album) and is typical Schubert it ought to tempt the singer to display it.

* * *

6*

Volume VII.

   An Mein Klavier (Schubart): (To My Piano.)

   The name of C. F. D. Schubart will always be gratefully remembered
by lovers of Franz Peter Schubert for he wrote the words of *Die
Forelle.*

   'Gentle piano, what pleasure you give. If I am alone I whisper my
feelings to you, and your silvery voice speaks peace to me.'

   It has been suggested, and with good reason, that the piano Schubert
refers to was not a piano as we know it but a clavichord, the gentlest
of all keyboard instruments. The accompaniment should, therefore, be
really modest. Only in the interlude between verses can the player
sing out discreetly and tenderly, though thankful that he has a modern
pianoforte under his fingers.

   Rests in the vocal line do not necessarily make it incumbent on
the singer to use them uniformly for taking breath; these rests of
course are observed but the fact that no breath is taken tends to give an
over-all feeling of continuity and smoothness.

   On our record we used the postlude as an introduction and omitted
the fourth verse.

★ ★ ★

An den Frühling (Schiller): (To Spring.)

   The young god of spring, laden with his basket of flowers is welcomed joyfully by the lover who wants a rich garland for his sweetheart.

   Fresh and artless, the vocal line is made as *legato* as can be over the
pizzicato accompaniment. The Schubertian repetition of the last line
of each quatrain is particularly charming, especially on the bar before
the interlude (*Entgegen dir zu gehn* and *du, du giebstes mir*) when the
singer adopts for the only time the dancing rhythmic pattern of the
pianoforte's lilting solo.

   There are three verses (six quatrains) to this strophic song but
Fischer-Dieskau sings only the first two.

★ ★ ★

An die Entfernte (Goethe): (To the Distant Beloved.)

   Goethe's heart-wringing lines awakened the composer's deep
emotion. Now impassioned, now numbed by a ceaseless craving, they
bear us along on a tide of torment which Schubert expresses with
unadorned directness.

'So have I really lost you, my lovely? I call on you to return, Oh beloved, come back to me.'

We are arrested immediately by the lover's urgency in the falling vocal line and our misgivings as to the response have already been aroused in the pianoforte introduction by the warning note of E flat and the diminished sevenths. *So hab'ich* in the singer's opening phrase are anacruses leading to *wirklich* (truly) which is the crucial point, therefore the note on *So* (a high G) is not *attacked* in the accepted sense.

Through a succession of keys the tortured quest, pursued up to the despairing *O komm, Geliebte, mir zurück!* (Oh, come beloved, come back to me) is repeated again and again always with more despair and heightened pitch.

The postlude duplicates the introduction. Two bars are added for the final cadence and, alas, the discordant E flat sounds the expiry of hope.

★ ★ ★

Nachtviolen (Mayrhofer): (Dame's Violets.)

When flowers were his theme Schubert handled them with a feminine tenderness which reflected his love of them—the touching retrospection in *Frühlingstraum, Ich träumte von bunten Blumen* (I dreamt of bright flowers) (*Winterreise*); his miller lad's *die Blümlein am Ufer, die Blauen, sie nickten und blickten ihr nach* (the small blue brookside flowers gazed and nodded back) in *Tränenregen*; *Viola* where his enthusiasm led him to some length (unjustifiable length according to some Schubertians, but not to me) all bear eloquent testimony that the beauty of a little wild flower, a hedge rose perhaps, touched a chord in this Arcadian.

The fancy of the poet in *Nachtviolen* to plunge himself into the velvety blue bank of Dame's violets is enough for Schubert to bequeath to us two pages of soft radiance. Yes, continually soft, ever *legato*, the voice is suspended like a blossom on its slender stem, high in the stave. The topmost notes in the vocal line are As and they are sung to the unimportant *dem—in dem sammten Blau* (in the soft blue) so on no account should they be emphasized. This applies equally to his high notes in the blithe second verse.

The third verse begins as if promising to be a repetition of the first but develops into a variation of surpassing loveliness to make a melodic duet with the pianoforte. Hitherto the accompaniment had remained consistently in the treble, hand in hand with the voice, but at the words *nun blüht in stummen Nächten fort die heilige Verbindung* (in silent nights this sacred bond endures) the two part company, for the piano makes a slow descent spread over five bars into the bass, its leave-taking made with affectionate reluctance as suggested by the left hand's hesitating syncopation. The voice continues on its lofty plane with superimposed counterpoint or *obligato*, giving the impression of an improvisation. These are quivering moments, ineffably precious, and every time I hear the song I anticipate them with excitement.

Modified Rapture

I HAD intended to name this 'Hymn of Hate' to complement the title of the preceding chapter but could not entertain for long the thought of such exaggeration, for the sake of effect, levelled at the devoted head of Franz Peter Schubert.

There is, in any case, very little music that I hate, but the artist cannot invariably be so naïve as to love with equal enthusiasm each and every manner of music he is asked to perform.

Schumann's *Frauen Liebe und Leben* (Woman's Love and Life) is a tender and emotive cycle but the fact that there is one song in it I dislike is not sufficient reason for me to ask the singer to omit it.

Surely there are occasions when a painter will accept a commission for a portrait and find that his subject is uncongenial to him: this does not signify that his portrait will be a failure. Sir William Orpen's large oil of John McCormack was one of his best works, yet painter and sitter took an increasing dislike to each other at every sitting. The musician has a parallel with the painter in that he does not invariably find himself ardently enthusiastic over every piece of music that comes his way but tries all the more, professional that he is, to throw himself into it, telling himself that there is something missing in him (the performer) rather than an inadequacy on the composer's part. I have this experience when accompanying Schubert's *Sei mir gegrüsst* (I Greet You). The Rückert lyric starts promisingly enough with 'O you, torn from me and my kiss, I greet you, I kiss you'. But the beloved sends greetings and kisses with awful tedium about twenty times throughout the song. Just when the music is working up hopefully to a new harmonic or emotional climax—perhaps even a fresh modulation—it sinks back (dejectedly in my opinion) to the identical tonic pattern of the greeting and the kissing. I am not posing as an *enfant terrible* nor does it give me pleasure to reveal my dislike, hitherto undisclosed, of the song, for it is a favourite with many Schubertians (in fact Richard Capell calls it a masterpiece), while the composer himself liked it so much that he used the theme in a set of variations for violin and pianoforte: *Fantasia* Op. 159. No, the inadequacy must be mine and I only declare it now in the hope that my lack of interest in the song is not apparent in my playing of it. Professional integrity may have pulled me through and above all have prevented my honoured partners Fischer-Dieskau and others from perceiving my lack of conviction. I certainly never enlightened them, it would have been inconsiderate and tactless to do so.

On the other hand, there are Schubert songs which are condemned and with reason, for their inordinate length. He could not leave Schiller alone and in his early days covered reams of manuscript with ballads—sometimes referred to as operas for voice and piano—such as *Der Taucher* (The Diver) and *Die Bürgschaft* (The Bond), they seem interminable—*Der Taucher* slightly the longer of the two is over twenty-three minutes long and covers twenty-four pages. There are stretches of fine writing in it but they hardly compensate for the arid patches and one feels regret that Schubert should have wasted time on it. In truth, the story of The Diver is childish, but the performers— and this is the rub—have to practise and rehearse it diligently because it is by no means childish to sing or to play. I am reminded of Vladimir Horowitz, the pianist, asking Artur Schnabel why he did not play the Liszt Sonata and getting the reply (Schnabel did not like Liszt) 'Because I should have to practise it.'

Schiller's *libretto* tells of the mediaeval king attended by his court and his fair daughter, who throws a jewelled chalice deep down into the 'boiling, steaming, roaring, hissing' whirlpool of Charybdis, and offers him who recovers it, possession of the prize. After a certain lack of response from the royal retinue, a handsome youth comes forward and dives into the deep abyss, and to the joy of the multitude at last emerges clutching the glittering prize. Scarce giving the intrepid diver time to recover his breath, the king demands an account of his submarine adventure and the boy describes the sharks, salamanders, dragons whose gaping jaws menaced him on every side. Alas, for the hero, his picturesque eloquence surpasses his discretion for the royal curiosity is re-awakened—once more the gracious monarch hurls the goblet into the swirling waters. 'Retrieve it and you shall have my daughter's hand in marriage.' The court is aghast, the princess implores her father to have done with his fun but to no avail. Again the youth dives and is seen no more. (I picture the crowd as they disperse shouting with undiminished fervour 'Long live the king.')

The young Schubert, you may be sure, had darting semiquaver

chromatics, gurgling basses in the pianoforte to reinforce the singer's narrative.

A German friend of mine tells me that at her school when asked to describe Schiller's *Der Taucher* and his cruel end, the girl's answer was *Gluck! Gluck! Weg war er* (Glug! Glug! He was gone).

Curiously enough I do not find the song so boring to play as *Sei mir gegrüsst* for the many changes in tempo and the rapid passage work, though not very difficult, keep the pianist on the alert.

Is the composer's judgement to be trusted so far as his own work is concerned with every goose a swan and every lass a queen? This question arises when Schubert's *Einsamkeit* (Solitude) is considered. I am referring to Mayrhofer's setting of 1818—not to be compared or confused with the Müller setting in *Die Winterreise*. It is seventeen pages long and takes eighteen minutes to sing. There is superb music in each of the six verses but the structure has six different styles, each scene, if I may so describe each verse, being connected by recitative. When I listen to Fischer-Dieskau's performance on our record I am carried away by it but I am on Capell's side when he describes the song as unpractical. The poem tells of a youth attracted to monastic life, tempted in turn by the world, by a longing for companionship, for carnal pleasure, and who at last finds peace (dear Schubert!) in the woodland, with its running stream and its cuckoo.

Schubert was on holiday when he wrote enthusiastically to his Viennese friends '*Einsamkeit* is the best thing I have done so far'. I think the sentence should have continued 'so far, on this holiday' and feel sure that is what was intended.

In any case, unpractical for recital purposes though it may be, the student would do well to study *Einsamkeit* for it contains much that is thoroughbred Schubert.

My dislike of *Die Liebe hat gelogen* (Love Has Lied) and *Du liebst mich nicht* (You Do Not Love Me) is quite unreasonable but none the less seminal. I cannot imagine any composer dealing any better with these poems than Schubert, the music is heartfelt yet I find the sentiment in each song maudlin. The memory of a much-admired singer, many years ago, wringing her hands in anguish as she sang *Du liebst mich nicht* has turned me against the song and I cannot hear it without this overdrawn picture coming to my mind.

My aversions are catholic and are distributed impartially among the great masters; for instance I cannot bear the cumbersome flapping of *O liebliche Wangen* (O, Sweet Cheeks), Brahms must have had the Lobster Quadrille in mind when he wrote it. *Botschaft* (Message)

Wehe, Lüftchen, lind und lieblich um die Wange der Geliebten (Blow, breeze, gentle and loving about the cheek of my beloved) looks on paper like a cavalry charge and needs all the pianist's skill to prevent it sounding like one, for the accompaniment is thick and situated in the most resonant part of the instrument. It would indeed be admirable as a movement for violin and piano but is an infelicitous consort for the gentle breeze of the lyric.

I am a lover of Brahms—all his work and most of his songs—but perhaps it was this side of him as evinced in the two songs I have quoted that repelled Benjamin Britten.

Hugo Wolf had his failures though not so many, but as for Richard Strauss, so far as I am concerned—nearly all the songs where he resorts to broad comedy can be thrown away.

In presuming to inveigh against one or two Schubert songs I am only expressing a personal opinion, but when he is subjected to an attack such as Sir Hubert Parry made in his *Art of Music*, I am scandalized:

> Schubert is conspicuous among great composers for the insufficiency of his musical education. . . . He had no great talent for self-criticism and the least possible feeling for abstract design, balance and order.

Schubert's design, almost invariably is perfectly balanced; his spiritual or abstract comprehension is arguably as high as any composer who ever lived (and certainly above the discernment of Parry); his simplicity would also be anathema to Sir Hubert, a few of whose songs are quite acceptable though contrived and always wanting in the divine fire. Lack of self-criticism? Perhaps if Schubert had been adequately blessed with even the barest necessities of life he might have forbidden the publication of some of his early works, an excuse which cannot be made on behalf of the middling composer who presumes to sit in judgement on the master.

'Mediocrity's supreme delight,' says Hans Keller, 'is genius going wrong.'

Retreat to Prepared Positions

IN THE prehistoric past *The Times* had a fourth leader which gave everybody so much pleasure and had been one of the features of the journal for so long that the management decided to expunge it. Any and every interesting subject came into its orbit provided it had originality and was elegantly written. The writers on the paper in those days were always anonymous; Bernard Darwin was a regular contributor as well as their incomparable golf correspondent. His daughter Nicola told me, 'You can generally identify my father because he so often quotes Dickens,' but his style was easily recognizable for he was an essayist of the highest distinction, with a grace, a subtle humour and a warm humanity that were captivating. One of his essays had cross-word puzzles for its theme. Now I do not believe for a moment that Bernard Darwin was addicted to this strange form of amusement, but he told an anecdote or reminiscence about it that I have always remembered. Apparently his tutor at Cambridge was a master at solving the difficult puzzle in *The Times*. (I do not complete it myself except on the rarest occasions and only then after having recourse to books of reference.) However, this particular hero, according to Darwin, solved this puzzle every morning without trouble and did it while his breakfast was being prepared; 'moreover he liked his eggs lightly boiled.'

The pungent afterthought, or shall we say appendix, though not necessarily a feature of Darwin's style closes the issue beyond argument.

Sir Winston Churchill was a past-master at it. When struck down by appendicitis during an election campaign (1922) in which he was defeated and the Government routed, he summed up the situation with flavour: 'In the twinkling of an eye I found myself without an office, without a seat, without a party, and without an appendix.'

And now in binary form I return to my theme.

The fact that I find myself in retirement sitting under the branches of a cherry tree in my garden in the Chiltern Hills penning these immortal lines is due to *The Times* crossword puzzle.

When we lived in London it was our habit after lunch—appointments permitting—to attempt to crack this nut. Enid has flashes of brilliance that have to be heard to be believed, but even when her concentration flags and her eyes stray from these mesmeric black and white squares, they stray to good effect, for they fastened one memorable day on an adjacent column where a property in Buckinghamshire was advertised. We drove out next day and after much difficulty found a woodman's cottage in deplorable condition surrounded by a wilderness of thistles and nettles: one stepped down into mud from its front door. But turning our backs resolutely on this elderly erection we looked over the tall undergrowth and despondent bean poles and beheld a *coup d'oeil* which captivated us and continues to do so after ten years of daily contemplation. I fell in love with it on the spot. Graham Sutherland declared that it is difficult to explain why you like a place: it is like describing a rice pudding. Let me say then, quite simply, that it was a study in varying shades of green; the greens of beech, of lime, oak and pasture, with undulating hills curving and folding into the distance. The big sloping field on the horizon, we discovered later, is called 'Stages'; at one time the stage coach crossed it on its way to Oxford. Not a brick, not a chimney-pot marred the scene, all was peace; no sound, only the trees whispering in the breeze; no movement, only the lazy cattle in the steep meadow drifting *molto lento* and without surprise across the grass. 'I could live here,' I said to Enid. This was enough and before I knew it she had arranged everything with the agents and an appointment was made with the architect.

About 200 years old, it is a flint cottage and its first occupant according to history had been a highwayman named Shrimpton whose practice was carried out on the London–Oxford road some four miles distant. This was as ideal a refuge for Mr. Shrimpton with his spoils as for me; in fact, with my taking possession the wheel can be said to have turned full circle—from one artful practitioner to another.

To say the place wanted renovating and enlarging would be putting it mildly, it needed not only a face lift but a major operation. As for the wilderness, turf must be put down where nettles and sprawling blackberry bushes had full sway. 'There will be plenty to do in the garden,' said Enid with relish, but that is all very well for her—she has green fingers. My thoughts instinctively flew to a friend who, dressed like a raggle-taggle gypsy when he was tending his hedges, was accosted one day by an elderly lady in a chauffeur-driven car and asked what he charged per hour; 'Madame, I have a special arrangement here. You see I sleep with the lady of the house.' Similar privileges come my way, it is true, but I could not metamorphose myself so suddenly into your complete gardener.

In the meantime we had to go to Japan and it was with excitement that we returned to see what progress had been made. To our dismay on opening the front door we saw that a stairway had been installed— bulky and pretentious, out of keeping with the surroundings but ideal for a baronial hall; it had to be pulled down; in its stead a staircase light and airy was placed and realigned.

It was in 1965 that we had to decide whether to have Beechwood Cottage, as we christened it, for a hiding place, making Hamilton Terrace—handed down in turn to us from Gina Bachauer, Elisabeth Schumann and Kathleen Ferrier—as our headquarters or, alluring alternative, to retire here as successors of the worthy Shrimpton and have a *pied-à-terre* in London, for it would be impossible to carry on with concerts, rehearsals and the concentrated work these entailed and live in the country as I had learned nearly twenty-five years previously when we lived at Box Hill in Surrey.

This was a handsome place, but the journey from north London took too long. Situated on a famous beauty spot the house commanded glorious views towards the South Downs but this unfortunately proved to be a drawback, for it attracted caravanners in such crowds that they had to be organized into camps. These were pitched in the hinterland, out of sight it is true, but of their proximity I was made uncomfortably aware when, on ordering delivery of our morning papers I was asked by the proprietress 'Which camp, dear?' Cold-hearted, phlegmatic Englishman that I am this form of address is unpleasing to me; it should only be used at the breakfast table by a couple who have not been formally introduced.

Another drawback was that we were exposed to all the winds that blew, and one could *see* with trepidation the weather coming. It is no wonder that I dislike Stanford's song *A Soft Day* with its 'and the rain drips, drips, drips, drips from the leaves' with the singer's sibilants whistling descriptively and depressingly: when the rain arrived at Box Hill it hissed as it attacked us, horizontally. Furthermore I am convinced that certain altitudes are unsuited to some people. I have been as happy as a sandboy at sea level and have lived for months in the mountains but on our balcony was engraved the words '700 feet above sea level'; I pointed it out with a proprietorial flourish to our guests while concealing a slight feeling of dyspepsia. Six hundred or eight hundred feet might have been perfect, but seven hundred—impossible. (No wonder Walter Legge called me the biggest prima donna in the business, though I reminded him that he was 'in the business' too.)

We shall always associate Brockham Warren with Kathleen Ferrier for she loved it and never tired of the glorious view, but when I compare it with Beechwood Cottage I know which I prefer. The one was imposing and rather austere, but this place is charming, warm and friendly.

It dawned on me that I had arrived at the stage when I could put an end to concert work and foreign tours: fifty years was a good stretch of arduous professional striving and I wanted to take life easier or at least enjoy a different mode of living. I had no ambition to martyrize myself by expiring at a recital in the middle of some song. Imagine the annoyance of the singer having to carry on doggedly with 'Der Tod dass ist die kühle Nacht' (Death is the Cool Night) unaccompanied: a sensational valediction and not without a certain grandeur, with but one unsurmountable disadvantage—I should not be present next morning to read the headlines, if any.

Retirement and retreat from London were the order of the day and a flat was found in St. John's Wood to be used when we came up to enjoy concerts, theatres, and to see friends. And it was close to Lords.

In the course of twelve months we spent about three nights there all told, finding it much more to our liking to drive back to the country no matter how late the hour. It is an easy journey from London and we decided for the first time since I was twenty to have no address in town.

Most of my friends after I announced my retirement, and especially those who have visited us, applaud our decision to seek the rural quietude and the unpolluted air of the Chilterns. One or two of them cannot understand us at all and declare it would be impossible to exist so far away from Piccadilly Circus. Solomon, even though his first exclamation on his initial visit 'I *like* it' still rings in my ears, came to the conclusion that after two years we would be unable to resist the pull of London, even as we had quitted Box Hill. Emmie Tillett, the concert agent, whom I have known and worked with so congenially for nigh on sixty years (with the bearing and complexion of a woman half her age) wants to know what we do with ourselves all day. We asked her recently how she managed to look so well. 'By hard work,' she told us with a severe glance, as if we ought to be ashamed of ourselves.

Well, what do we do all day? The patient reader who has accompanied me thus far will know by the foregoing pages that my time during the past decade, since my official leave-taking of the concert platform, has not been unoccupied. Since my withdrawal to Buckinghamshire I have also written two books, and writing a book, no matter how inept the author, is a full-time occupation. I confess that the days when there are no adjudications or visits to London are red letter days and are all too short; filled by gardening, reading, listening to music. Then there are our walks, these are a theme with variations of Diabelli proportions and wherever we go we are greeted by the villagers and farm workers with cheery words: even the cows in the pasture no longer retreat at our approach, so familiar have we become to them. There is a Hereford bull in one of the herds, mild mannered and, so far as we are concerned, benevolent, but I have not attempted a Veronica pass with him.

Dietrich Fischer-Dieskau on his first visit to Beechwood Cottage declared with deliberation after surveying the prospect, 'You are a King' and I respect his judgement enough to accept it without demur. My realm extends over two acres and I have no further territorial ambitions.

So now we are country folk experiencing a peace of mind that neither of us has known for many years.

It would not suit everybody, no good for the young, striving to win; too withdrawn for him who simply must be seen on the 'important occasion' but wonderfully harmonious for me. It is only made possible by one supernal blessing for which I never, never cease to be thankful—perfect companionship.

Index